FIRST STEPS
in
Religious Education

Published in 2008, 2016
by Connor Court Publishing Pty Ltd.

(c) Brendan Hyde and Richard Rymarz, 2008.

All Rights Reserved.

Connor Court Publishing Pty Ltd

PO BOX 7257

Redland Bay QLD 4165

www.connorcourt.com

ISBN: 9781921421044

Front Cover-
iStockphoto- used with permission

Design -
Connor Court Publishing

Printed in Australia

FIRST STEPS
in
Religious Education

Brendan Hyde
Richard Rymarz

CONTENTS

PREFACE 1

CHAPTER 1: 3
The nature and purpose of religious education in Catholic schools

CHAPTER 2: 15
Revelation as a foundation for religious education

CHAPTER 3: 27
The human, religious and spiritual development of young children

CHAPTER 4: 41
Pedagogical influences on early years' religious education classrooms

CHAPTER 5: 55
Godly Play – a way of religious education for early years' settings

CHAPTER 6: 67
Planning for religious education: Looking at curriculum frameworks

CHAPTER 7: 79
What do I do if this happens? Dealing with some difficult issues in classroom religious education

CHAPTER 8: 91
Personal and liturgical prayer with early years' students

CHAPTER 9: 103
Teaching about sacraments

CHAPTER 10: 115
Dimensions of learning in religious education

Preface

TEACHING RELIGIOUS EDUCATION to children in their first years of formal schooling presents many challenges. For most, religion is not a part of their childhood experience. Often, young children come to school from families who, for various reasons, do not have a strong connection with their local faith community. The majority of these children have neither a language for speaking about religion, nor any experiences of religion, at least none that can be remembered.

First Steps in Religious Education is an interactive handbook designed to assist those preparing to teach religious education in early years' classrooms and to address these challenges. It also provides a sound general introduction to religious education in the Catholic primary school context, with a focus on early years' settings. Through a balance of theory and practice, the reader-participants are led to consider the nature and purpose of religious education, and to begin to develop a personal vision of themselves as teachers of religious education.

Both authors have been highly experienced and successful teachers of religious education in Catholic schools, and are effective teacher educators in the discipline. This book is infused with their experience and knowledge.

Beginning with a consideration of the nature and purpose of religious education in Catholic schools and an investigation of the concept of Revelation, this book proceeds to explore some of the pertinent issues facing religious educators in early years' settings: the human, religious and spiritual development of young children, pedagogical influences on early years religious education programs, as well as methodological considerations. There are also useful chapters which examine difficult issues and questions in religious education, as well as teaching about Sacraments and providing opportunities for prayer with students in their early years' of schooling. These chapters provide a mix of content and processes that will enhance the work of the teacher of religious education in early years' settings.

We offer *First Steps in Religious Education* as a guide and resource for your continuing development as religious educators.

Brendan Hyde
Richard Rymarz

CHAPTER 1

THE NATURE AND PURPOSE OF RELIGIOUS EDUCATION IN CATHOLIC SCHOOLS

Activity 1.1
I think the role of Religious Education in a Catholic school should be ...
Complete this sentence and provide a justification for what you have written.

HISTORICAL INSIGHT

Below is the introduction to Book 4 of the *My Way to God* series published in 1964 and authorised for use in Catholic primary schools all over Australia.

Dear Child of God
When people go on a journey, they take a map or a guidebook. They look out for signposts. Often they take a guide who will show them the way.
We are on a journey. We are the New People of God, called by our Heavenly Father to make a journey to heaven. Yes, we are all on the Great March to the real Promised Land.
How are we to get there?
Are there any signposts? Is there a guidebook to tell us about the place we are going to and what to expect on the way?
Is there someone who can lead the way?
Yes, our loving Father has given us all these helps. The most wonderful of all is the Guide He has given us – His own Divine Son, Jesus Christ. If we follow Him we cannot get lost. We cannot see Him, but He speaks to us through the Church.
So, this year, while we work and pray and sing together on the Great March, we put our hand in Christ's and let Him lead us to the Father.

My Way to God, Sydney: EJ Dwyer, 1969, p. 4–5.

Questions:
1. *What images does this reading conjure up in your mind?*
2. *What does it tell you about Religious Education in this era?*
3. *What does it tell you about the students in this era?*

There are many ways of tackling how Religious Education should be approached in a contemporary Catholic primary school. The authors of *My Way to God*, for example, used the metaphor of Religious Education as providing a sure pathway to God for those who had already committed to making this journey. To focus this discussion let's examine formal Religious Education more closely; that is, Religious Education as it is taught to students in a classroom setting. This is not to say that Religious Education does not have any other manifestations in the school, but this aspect will be discussed later. In contemporary literature Religious Education has a number of purposes and goals. There is tension between catechesis and the educational dimensions of Religious Education. Tension should not have connotations of a negative fruitless struggle but should be seen as something which gives vitality and direction to the discussion.

WHAT IS CATECHESIS?

Catechesis can be defined in a number of ways. Before looking at some of these definitions it is important to distinguish catechetical instruction. In Australia as well as many other countries prior to the 1960s the dominant form of religious instruction in schools followed a directed and didactic format. The situation has often been described as being based on memorisation and rote learning. The reality was a little more complex, but it is fair to say that catechetical instruction in this era was very teacher-centred and relied heavily on the question and answer format of the catechism. Catechism here refers to local catechism produced in large numbers, not the authoritative Roman Catechism.

So if catechesis is not directed instruction based on learnt answers to set questions, what is it? One key way of describing catechesis is as a dialogue between believers. Another is to describe it as all that is done to make a person a better follower of Jesus. Both these definitions rely on the person already being a believer or a member of an active faith community. To become a better follower of Jesus, for example, assumes that you are already a follower.

Catholic schools have an important role to play in catechesis. This is especially true in primary schools, which are usually where students complete the sacraments of Initiation – Eucharist and Confirmation, and also celebrate the sacrament of Reconciliation. These sacraments are certainly directed to enriching the faith lives of students. Having said this, however, the pre-eminent place for catechesis is not the Catholic school but the family. This is where faith is most likely to be strengthened and nurtured. The school's role is complementary here. If catechesis is not occurring in the home the school cannot adequately substitute for this. It can play an educational role but it cannot replace the lived experience of faith.

EDUCATIONAL GOALS

The fact that many students in Catholic schools and other Christian schools today do not have a strong connection to an active faith community means that an approach to Religious Education cannot be entirely centred on catechesis. Another way of looking at Religious Education then places the priority on the educative aspects of the discipline. If we assume that a critical aspect of the school's role is to educate students and to focus on a growth in knowledge then we can follow this logic in Religious Education. In Catholic school classrooms the goal of Religious Education is to help students build up their understanding of the Catholic Tradition in a way that is educationally sound and sophisticated. This goal is not opposed to catechesis; rather it is complementary to it. Religious

Education therefore should adopt the same language and rigour of other subject disciplines. Teaching and learning activities that are used in other areas should be directly applicable to Religious Education. Assessment should be used and should have the same scope and depth as in other parts of the school's curriculum.

Activity 1.2

A strategy for teaching about the Trinity is given below. It is an example of an educational strategy in Religious Education. How would you evaluate this approach?

Step	Description
Recognition	Make a clear commitment to teach hard topics, such as the Trinity, in the curriculum. This does not mean that every lesson should involve such themes, but teachers should have a firm realisation that these will arise and should be planned for.
Orientation	Examine the existing curriculum to see where the Trinity has been covered in the past. Also recognise that it may be covered again in the future. Hard topics, such as the Trinity, often require a number of treatments in a four or six year program. Ask yourself what aspect of the topic will be covered here and what will be done later. Be aware of the age and prior learning of students.
Research	Identify a number of key resources in the area. These can be divided into two types. Firstly, teaching resources used by others to teach the Trinity. Secondly, sources that help teachers understand the Trinity. Be aware that a good deal can be achieved here by some guided selective reading.

Focus	Working with others try to encapsulate as briefly as possible the heart of the issue. What is it that makes the Trinity hard and why do students have trouble understanding it? What is their thinking about the issues involved and, especially, what common misconceptions exist?
Response	Repeat the focus step but now try to encapsulate the Christian teaching on the Trinity that you want to convey to the students.
Educational Goals	Using outcome language or similar write down what you expect of students who have completed this unit of work. Some teachers may prefer to do this step after completing the teaching strategies step which follows.
Teaching strategies	This is the critical step. Here a series of teaching and learning activities that will engage students are developed. Rely here on your knowledge as a skilled teacher. Give some thought to how many lessons you are going to devote to the topic. Also plan assessment strategies that will enhance the learning of the students. The outline for the unit begins this process with some suggested teaching and learning experiences and assessment strategies.
Review and consolidation	Try to make some judgement as to the success of your lesson sequence and record what was successful. Also start to develop a pool of resources that have been helpful so that when this topic is tackled again you have a starting point.

Source document 1.

The Religious Dimension of Education in a Catholic School.

There is a close connection, and at the same time a clear distinction, between religious instruction and catechesis, or the handing on of the Gospel message. The close connection makes it possible for a school to remain a school and still integrate culture with the message of Christianity. The distinction comes from the fact that, unlike religious instruction, catechesis presupposes that the hearer is receiving the Christian message as a salvific reality. Moreover, catechesis takes place within a community living out its faith at a level of space and time not available to a school: a whole lifetime.

The aim of catechesis, or handing on the Gospel message, is maturity: spiritual, liturgical, sacramental and apostolic; this happens most especially in a local Church community. The aim of the school, however, is knowledge. While it uses the same elements of the Gospel message, it tries to convey a sense of the nature of Christianity, and of how Christians are trying to live their lives. It is evident, of course, that religious instruction cannot help but strengthen the faith of a believing student, just as catechesis cannot help but increase one's knowledge of the Christian message.

The distinction between religious instruction and catechesis does not change the fact that a school can and must play its specific role in the work of catechesis. Since its educational goals are rooted in Christian principles, the school as a whole is inserted into the evangelical function of the Church. It assists in and promotes faith education.

RDECS, 68–69.

In your own words explain the distinction between catechesis and religious instruction.

Questions:

1. What role does Religious Education play in catechesis?
2. What do you think the aim of a Catholic school is?
3. What are the implications for teachers in early years' religious education classrooms?

Activity 1.3:

Three students in an early years' class.

Imagine that you are teaching an RE class and in your grade are the following three students. Barry is new to the school, having transferred from a government school. He is not a Catholic and has trouble articulating his beliefs and values. He describes himself as a Christian because that is what his grandmother told him. Barry is not an isolated example. The non-Catholic enrolment in Catholic schools continues to grow, and in most Australian dioceses exceeds 20%. Many non-Catholic students also enrol in Catholic schools in countries such as Canada. Sandra is a Catholic but has a loose and distant affiliation with the Church. She would be typical of many students in Catholic schools today. Her family sometimes goes to church at Easter or Christmas. Brendan comes from a committed Catholic family who are active in their parish. He is part of a parish-based youth group and regularly prays on his own and with his family.

Questions:

1. How do you think the three students mentioned above will respond to your lesson?
2. Do the backgrounds of the three students make a coherent approach to Religious Education impossible?
3. What should be your goal for the lesson?

Taking an example from the contemporary classroom is a good way of illustrating how actions such as catechesis and Religious Education can interact. Imagine a teacher in a Catholic school is teaching about the sacraments. Let us assume that she takes an educational approach to this. The emphasis in the classroom is teaching about the sacraments, learning about their origins, what they signify and why they are important to Catholics. She will use a variety of teaching and learning strategies to present the topic, she will use conventional educational assessments, and this topic will be part of a well integrated and spiral curriculum.

How students receive this topic depends greatly on where they are on their life-long faith journey. Take a student who is part of an active faith community and has made some type of personal commitment to following Jesus. This student may receive these lessons as genuine catechesis; that is, this teaching is contributing to making the student a better follower of Jesus. Learning about the sacraments is a good way of consolidating and nurturing faith development. This follows the principle from Thomas Aquinas that the more we know about our faith the more we come to love and treasure it.

Another student, however, may not have the same background as the first student. This person may be more distant from their faith community and, while a baptised Catholic, has not really developed or lived out their baptismal promises. For this student the educational focus of the lesson will contribute to their understanding of the sacraments. It may also spark an interest in finding out more about them, leading to a personal faith response some time in the future. What is true of this student is also very relevant to those students in the class who are not Catholics and who may have a poor grasp of Catholic beliefs.

In the case of the second student the Religious Education class could have an evangelistic impact. Evangelisation, strictly speaking, is the proclamation of the Word to those who have not heard it. When you evangelise someone you proclaim to them the good news about Jesus. This is more than just telling them about Jesus. You try to introduce them to the reality of Jesus acting in the world and acting in their lives. Normally when you speak about evangelisation you are talking about a process that is initiatory; that is, it is something new. Given our current culture we can expand our definition to talk about the evangelisation of people who have heard about Jesus in the past but have had very little lived experience of an active faith community. This so-called New Evangelisation would include those who are canonical members of the faith community; that is, they are baptised, but are not active. Students in their first years of formal schooling could often be included here.

Note that the goal in both cases above is educational, focusing on a growth in understanding about Religious Education. How this is received depends on the student and other support mechanisms in the schools, and also the parish.

SOURCE DOCUMENT 2:

The Catholic School on the Threshold of the Third Millennium.

On the threshold of the Third Millennium education faces new challenges which are the result of a new socio-political and cultural context. First and foremost, we have a crisis of values which, in highly developed societies in particular, assumes the form, often exalted by the media, of subjectivism, moral relativism and nihilism. The extreme pluralism pervading contemporary society leads to behaviour patterns which are at times so opposed to one another as to undermine any idea of community identity. Rapid structural changes, profound technical innovations and the globalisation of the economy affect human life more and more throughout the world. Rather than prospects of development for all, we witness the widening of the gap between rich and poor, as well as massive migration from underdeveloped to highly-developed countries. The phenomena of multiculturalism and an increasingly multi-ethnic and multi-religious society is at the same time an enrichment and a source of further problems. To this we must add, in countries of long-standing evangelisation, a growing marginalisation of the Christian faith as a reference point and a source of light for an effective and convincing interpretation of existence.

CSTTM, 1.

Questions:

1. *Define the following: subjectivism, moral relativism and nihilism.*
2. *Do you agree that in developed societies we have a crisis of values?*
3. *In your own words explain this quote: '... in countries of long-standing evangelisation, a growing marginalisation of the Christian faith as a reference point and a source of light for an effective and convincing interpretation of existence'.*

SOME CHALLENGES TO RELIGIOUS EDUCATION IN SCHOOLS

***Case Study 1**:* The place of Religious Education in the curriculum.

Reaction statement: Religious Education permeates all aspects of what we do in a Catholic school. It is present not just in Religious Education classes but throughout the syllabus.

Wendy on the place of Religious Education: *We try to bring Religious Education into everything we do rather than focus on it as a separate subject. It permeates everything that we do in a Catholic school. It is present across all subject disciplines; the students almost imbue it in all they do.*

Questions:

1. *React to Wendy's statement.*

A pressure on all schools today is what can be called the crowed curriculum. There is an enormous expectation on schools to provide a range of programs. If Religious Education is part of every program there is a danger that it will be part of no program.

Core Statement: In an educational model, Religious Education needs to be explicit and this is usually best achieved if it has its own place in the curriculum. This is not to discount Religious Education permeating all subjects but this seems to work best if this sits alongside a strong distinctive Religious Education programs.

***Case Study 2**:* Respecting the scope and limitations of Religious Education.

Reaction statement: Religious Education in schools should result in an increase in the religious practice of students.

Brad on the place of Religious Education: *You know, it's hard; we try to give a really good RE program in the school, we revise it to try to make it as interesting and relevant as possible. It just doesn't work. None of these kids goes to church on Sunday.*

Questions:

1. *React to Brad's statement.*

As spelled out in *Catechesi Tradendae* Catholic schools have a clear role to play in catechesis, which is a focus on nurturing and developing the faith of the believer. Indeed, Catholic schools do offer many opportunities for catechesis, such as school liturgies and faith-based support groups. In the classroom Religious Education is centred on increase in knowledge. It is hoped that this may result in a maturing of faith response by students. At the same time it must be recognised that the most important place for catechesis is the faith community, which for most students is their family. If catechesis is not taking place in the family then the school cannot compensate for this.

SOURCE DOCUMENT 3:

Apostolic Exhortation Catechesi Tradendae of Pope John Paul II – On Catechesis in Our Time.

In view of practical difficulties, attention must be drawn to some of the characteristics of this instruction:
- *It must be systematic, not improvised but programmed to reach a precise goal;*
- *It must deal with essentials, without any claim to tackle all disputed questions or to transform itself into theological research or scientific exegesis;*
- *It must nevertheless be sufficiently complete, not stopping short at the initial proclamation of the Christian mystery such as we have in the kerygma;*
- *It must be an integral Christian initiation, open to all the other factors of Christian life.*

CT 21

Questions:

1. *What do you think are some of the essentials of Religious Education?*
2. *How can Religious Education be programmed?*
3. *What point is being made about Religious Education and disputed questions?*

FURTHER QUESTIONS AND ACTIVITIES

1. Sally, a teacher in an early years' classroom is taking her class of students to the Church for a prayer celebration. Is this an example of religious education or catechesis?
2. With a partner, devise two activities with could be classified as religious education and two that could be classified as catechetical. Justify your classifications.
3. Describe an instance which could be indicative of New Evangelisation.

RERERENCES

Congregation for Catholic Education. (1988). *The Religious Dimension of Education in a Catholic School: Guidelines for Reflection and Renewal.* Homebush, NSW: St Paul Publications.

Congregation for Catholic Education. (1998). *The Catholic School on the Threshold of the Third Millennium.* Homebush, NSW: St Paul Publications.

Pope John Paul II. (1979). *Apostolic Exhortation: Catechesi Tradendae.* Homebush, NSW: St Paul Publications.

CHAPTER 2

REVELATION AS A FOUNDATION FOR RELIGIOUS EDUCATION

SOURCE DOCUMENT 1:

Gaudium et Spes. **Pastoral Constitution on the Church in the Modern World.**

The Church has always had the duty of scrutinising the signs of the times and of interpreting them in the light of the Gospel. Thus, in language intelligible to each generation, she can respond to the perennial questions which men ask about this present life and the life to come, and about the relationship of the one to the other. We must therefore recognise and understand the world in which we live, its explanations, its longings, and its often dramatic characteristics.

GS, 4

Questions:

1. *What are some of the signs of the times?*
2. *For religious educators why is it important to understand the world that students live in?*
3. *How is reading the signs of the times informed by the Church's understanding of its own mission?*

Activity 2.1: *What is your understanding of the term revelation, and how does this influence the way that religious education is taught in a Catholic school?*

SOURCES OF REVELATION

Revelation, or taking away the veil, is the term used to describe the disclosure by God of what was previously hidden or unknown. It is the great theme of the Conciliar constitution *Dei Verbum* (Word of God).

Background to *Dei Verbum*

The Second Vatican Council was the watershed event for Catholicism in the twentieth century. The Council, essentially a meeting convened by the Pope and attended by all of the bishops of the Catholic Church, was the first general Council in a hundred years, and only one of twenty-one such councils in two millennia of Christian history. Ecumenical Councils are, therefore, very significant events in the life of the Church. Teachings of Councils are extremely important and carry great authority. The Second Vatican Council was held between 1962 and 1965 and met over four sessions. The Council was called by Blessed Pope John XXIII, who died after the first session, and was concluded by his successor Pope Paul VI. The Council produced sixteen documents. The four most important were the Constitutions, one of which, the *Dogmatic Constitution on Divine Revelation; Dei Verbum,* was realised on 18 November 1965 (the popular name *Dei Verbum*, as with many Roman documents, is derived from the dominant Latin phrase in the first sentence of the document).

If we consider revelation to be the free disclosure of God, then the most perfect form of revelation was in the person of Jesus Christ, what *Dei Verbum* calls the climax of divine self revelation. Theologians sometimes describe the time up until about the end of the first century of the common era as a time of foundational revelation. Revelation, in this sense, was complete in the person of Christ. Nothing can be added to this. The first disciples of Jesus then needed some time to reflect on and make sense of the events that had recently occurred. In this period the Scriptures were written and the cornerstones of the Church's self-understanding were established. There is no new revelation possible outside these foundations. Our understanding of the revelation in Christ can improve and get more profound but will never be complete. One can speak, therefore, about revelation in a future sense; not as if something is missing but when the fullness of revelation is manifested to us in what *Dei Verbum* calls the glorious manifestation of our Lord, Jesus Christ, that is still to come. St Paul in his First Letter to the Corinthians uses the analogy of our current understanding of God as being like looking into a dim mirror: this is contrasted with seeing God, at the culmination of our redemption, face to face.

There is also a sense that revelation is current. Just as the disciples of Jesus wrestled with questions about what it was that they had witnessed, and were changed by this, Christians today are exposed to revelation as something that can radically transform and recast lives. In the language of the Church this is a salvific reality – something which can shape our relationship with God. In this sense revelation is not a set of propositions that we must accept but is an event that we are invited to participate in, in response to God's self-revelation.

Source document 2:

Dei Verbum. Dogmatic Constitution on Divine Revelation.

For there is a growth in the understanding of the realities and the words which have been handed down. This happens through the contemplation and study made by believers, who treasure these things in their hearts (see Luke 2:19, 51), through a penetrating understanding of the spiritual realities which they experience, and through the preaching of those who have received through episcopal succession the sure gift of truth. For as the centuries succeed one another, the Church constantly moves forward towards the fullness of divine truth until the words of God reach their complete fulfillment in her.

The words of the holy fathers witness to the presence of this living tradition, whose wealth is poured into the practice and life of the believing and praying Church. Through the same tradition the Church's full canon of the sacred books is known, and the sacred writings themselves are more profoundly understood and unceasingly made active in her; and thus God, who spoke of old, uninterruptedly converses with the bride of His beloved Son; and the Holy Spirit, through whom the living voice of the Gospel resounds in the Church, and through her, in the world, leads unto all truth those who believe and makes the word of Christ dwell abundantly in them.

DV, 8.

Questions:

1. What is the Church constantly moving forward towards?
2. What is described here as the living tradition?
3. How is Scripture described?

RELATIONSHIP BETWEEN TRADITION AND SCRIPTURE

If revelation can be described as the self-revelation of God, the task of communicating this revelation is central to the mission of the Church. We can come to know about God through Scripture, the living tradition of the Church, and through careful reflection on our lives and the world we find ourselves in.

Activity 2.2: *What do you think is more important in religious education: Tradition or Scripture?*

The idea that Scripture and Tradition are in conflict in communicating God's revelation is a mistake. Both complement each other. The *Catechism of the Catholic Church* clearly sates that 'Both Scripture and Tradition must be accepted and honoured with equal sentiments of devotion and reverence' (82). *Dei Verbum* eloquently uses the image of both being mirrors in which we contemplate God. Both make up critical parts of the content of RE in Catholic schools.

Background to the Bible

There are many reasons for using Scripture in RE classes. It makes tangible and accessible core elements of students' faith and allows access to the earliest faith communities – their theology and practice. Using Scripture brings us closer to the words, actions and accorded teachings of Jesus. Not to do so is to deny students a key experience of their faith tradition. The more background the teachers have the more likely they are to open up some of the riches of the Scriptures to students.

The Bible is divided into two parts, the Old and New Testaments. The Old Testament (Hebrew Scriptures) contains the story, law and beliefs of the People of Israel. The first five books of the Old Testament, known as the Pentateuch, are the most sacred text of the Jewish tradition. The New Testament (Christian Scriptures) gives the story of Jesus and his early followers. The books of the Old Testament can be divided into four groups: Pentateuch, Historical, Prophets and Wisdom. The books of the New Testament can also be grouped: Gospels, The Acts of the Apostles, The Letters of St Paul, Letters and Revelation.

The Bible describes a period that covers over 2000 years of history. It begins with the calling of Abraham to leave the place of his birth and establish a new home in the land promised to him by God. The Bible mentions such events as the rise and fall of empires, the construction of the first Temple by King Solomon and the defeat and exile of the people of Israel at the hands of the Babylonians. The New Testament presents Jesus' birth, his teaching and his death and Resurrection. It concludes with the writings of the first Christian leaders in the latter part of the first century.

The Bible was written by many people. We often know little about the authors, although the message and significance of what they wrote is much clearer. The Bible was written over a thousand-year timeframe. The earliest writings in the Old Testament date to over 1000 years before the birth of Christ. The latest writings in the New Testament were completed sometime around 90CE.

What makes the Bible so important is that it is inspired writing. The Catholic Church teaches that God inspired the authors of the

Bible to use their own skills, talents and experiences to reveal the divine plan of salvation. The fact that God chose to inspire people to write the books of the Bible tells us something about God. Through the talents and abilities of people God is made known. The Bible invites human beings to enter into a living relationship with God.

The Catholic Church teaches that what is presented in the Bible is true. The Bible tells the truth about God and the plan of salvation. It does this in a number of ways. It is important to remember that to describe something as true is different from exactly retelling an event. All the books of the Bible had human authors, inspired by God but using their own talents and abilities. They may have presented a truth about God in a form that was not simply describing an event. For example, some of the psalms describe God as a shepherd. Is this true? Yes, it describes the great love and care that God has for all of us. Is it exact? No, God does not have a staff and look after sheep. The Bible was never intended to be a scientific account of events.

The Catholic Church teaches that the Word of God is revealed in the tradition of the Church and in the Bible. The Sacred Scriptures and the Sacred Tradition are like a mirror in which the Church contemplates God. The New Testament writings came out of a believing community, so the Church and the Bible have been closely linked since the earliest days of Christianity. But the Church existed before the Bible took its final form. The Bible is not a single book but a collection of books. The Bible is like a library. Like any library it contains different types of books.

But in order to keep the Gospel forever whole and alive within the Church, the apostles left bishops as their successors, 'handing over' to them 'the authority to teach in their own place'. This sacred tradition, therefore, and Sacred Scripture of both the Old and New Testaments are like a mirror in which the pilgrim Church on earth looks at God, from whom she has received everything, until she is brought finally to see Him as He is, face to face (see 1 John 3: 2).

DV, 7

Questions:

In the quotation above from Dei Verbum:
1. How is the relationship between Scripture and Tradition described?
2. Who are described as the successors of the apostles?
3. How is the fullness of revelation described?

When describing the teaching of the Church it is important to recognise that this is a living tradition that comes to us through the thought and deliberation of many years. Even before there was a canon of Scripture in the formal sense there was a believing community that had in itself a sense of the authority that came to its leaders through their connection with the apostles. In the rich teaching history of the Church there are a number of teachings which are of the utmost importance. An example of such a teaching can be found in the Creeds such as the Nicean and Apostolic Creeds.

Scripture and Tradition

SOURCE DOCUMENT 3:

Catechism of the Catholic Church

Sacred Scripture is the speech of God as it is put down in writing under the breath of the Holy Spirit. And Holy Tradition transmits in its entirety the Word of God which has been entrusted to the apostles by Christ the Lord and the Holy Spirit. It transmits it to the successors of the apostles so that, enlightened by the Spirit of Truth, they may faithfully preserve, expound and spread it abroad by their preaching. As a result the Church, to whom the transmission and interpretation of revelation is entrusted, 'does not derive her certainty about all revealed truths from the holy Scriptures alone. Both Scripture and Tradition must be accepted and honoured with equal sentiments of devotion and reverence.

CCC, 81–82

As a result the Church, to whom the transmission and interpretation of revelation is entrusted, 'does not derive her certainty about all revealed truths from the holy Scriptures alone'.

Questions:

1. How is Sacred Scripture described?
2. In your own words describe what 'Holy Tradition' is.
3. From where else does the Church get her certainty about revealed truth?

THE DYNAMISM OF REVELATION

Activity 2.3: *Can we discover God in the created universe? Think this question over and if you have the opportunity discuss it with someone else. Write down the main points that have come up in your reflections.*

God, the beginning and end of all things, can be known with certainty from created reality by the light of human reason, but teaches that it is through His revelation that those religious truths which are by their nature accessible to human reason can be known by all men with ease, with solid certitude and with no trace of error, even in this present state of the human race.

DV, 6

Questions:

1. Describe, in your own words, the main message in the quotation above. Do you agree with this?
2. What is described above as being accessible to human reason?
3. What implication does this have for the teaching of religious education?

One of the main messages reinforced by *Dei Verbum* is that we can come to know about God by using our reason and reflecting on the created world. This teaching can be seen in Scriptures such as the first chapter of Romans where the power of God is described as being clearly perceived in the created universe. Saying that we can come to an awareness of God through reason and reflection is more than just thinking about God when looking at a beautiful sunset. It is something about the human condition. If we look at the world around us, reflect on our own lives and ask what it is we really value then our minds naturally turn to the Creator God who brought all into being. Much of this type of thinking became prominent in Catholic circles immediately after the Second Vatican Council in the writings of, amongst others, Gabriel Moran.

SOURCE DOCUMENT 4:

Gabriel Moran: Vision and Tactics

I cannot approach the non-believer or the child with the assumption that he has not been touched by God's grace. I cannot assume that my task is to fill an empty vessel or that I possess something with which the vessel is to be filled. I can only approach the other with an attitude of invitation that we take up the quest together for the God already active in our lives. If all creation speaks of God, then God is revealed in the 'letting be of being,' that is, in things simply being themselves, the more truly they reflect the glory of God. God's revelation is not a religious veneer on things nor a religious message to be injected into people.

V & T, 24

Questions:

1. Summarise in a sentence or two the main message of this extract.
2. What assumptions does Moran make about learners?
3. How does Moran describe revelation?

One of the great themes of RE in the modern era is the emphasis on trying to incorporate, wherever possible, the experiential world of the student. You will hear many times in the discussion around RE phrases like, 'students have to relate to it', 'we must make it relevant', 'it has to speak to the world of the child or adolescent'. All these sentiments are really a call to make sure that we use the experience of the learner wherever possible. This is good teaching or pedagogy as it helps to build up students' understanding by engaging their prior knowledge. Good teachers have always used the experience of their students whenever they can. This does not mean that the only thing covered in RE has to have some experiential referent, or that we rely on human experience too much. When integrated into a strong curriculum framework experiential learning has an invaluable place in contemporary practice. It also has a strong theological place, based on the understanding of how God is revealed. As described in *Dei Verbum* and elsewhere we can come to a better understanding of God by reflecting on our lives and the creation around us. By using our God-given intellects we can come to a deeper awareness of the mystery of revelation.

Activity 2.4: *What are some ways that you can engage the experiential world of students into your teaching and leaning activities? Are there any areas that students in early years' classrooms today may find difficult to describe or relate to? If so, how would you deal with this?*

FUTHER QUESTIONS AND ACTIVITIES

1. In your own words, briefly describe what is meant by the relationship between Scripture and Tradition.

2. Consider the stories of Creation from the Bible (Genesis 1- 2). What do you believe the truth of the story to be?

3. How and where might students in early years' classrooms experience the presence of God? Discuss with a partner, and provide some justification for your response.

4. What do you think the implications of Revelation are for teaching religious education in early years' classrooms?

REFERENCES

Catechism of the Catholic Church. (1994). Homebush, NSW: St Paul Publications.

Dei Verbum – Dogmatic Constitution on Divine Revelation. In A. Flannery, (Ed.), *The sixteen basic documents of Vatican Council II* (1996). Dublin: Dominican Publications.

Gaudium et Spes - Pastoral Constitution on the Church in the Modern World. In A. Flannery, (Ed.), *The sixteen basic documents of Vatican Council II* (1996). Dublin: Dominican Publications.

Moran, G. (1968). *Vision and tactics.* New York: Herder and Herder.

CHAPTER 3

THE HUMAN, RELIGIOUS AND SPIRITUAL DEVELOPMENT OF YOUNG CHILDREN

A scenario:

David is 5 years old. He attends, in this his first year of formal schooling, the local parish primary school, a short walk from where he lives. He comes from a family who has provided him with a safe and secure home environment. Although David's family do not attend Sunday Mass regularly, his teacher has noticed that he imitates the actions of the priest, and he attempts to say the prayers he is learning at school in the evenings at home. In her reflective journal, David's teacher has noted that he frequently displays a sense of wonder and awe at the smallest of things in the classroom, such as the "pet" spider one of the other children brought to school in a secure jar. As well, she has noticed the expression of joy and delight on his face when he plays on the adventure playground equipment. She remembers David's older sister Emma, whom she taught 4 years ago, and cannot help but notice how Emma no longer seems to delight in the simple things of life. To David's teacher, Emma, who was once very much like David in many ways, is now much more reserved. She has noticed that while David's sense of curiosity is aroused easily, and he likes to ask the existential questions, such as what happens when you die, Emma does not talk about such things, and tends to keep these kinds of questions to herself. Emma is, however, very interested in the stories of the Bible, and is developing an interest in the lives of some of the saints.

The above story about David and his older sister Emma tells us much about the ways in which these children are growing and developing. In this chapter we will investigate what is known about the human, religious and spiritual development of young children, and from this, discern some implications for religious education in early years' classrooms?

Activity 3.1: *In the story above, which elements specifically would you consider to reveal something about the human development, the religious development, and spiritual development of David and his older sister Emma?*

HUMAN DEVELOPMENT

During the course of the last 100 years, cognitive psychology has taught us much about the way in which children develop. For example, French psychologist Jean Piaget explored and described hierarchically how people develop cognitively. Similarly, others, such as Lawrence Kohlberg have described the moral stages of development through which people pass throughout their lifespan. While the work of these theorists has been critiqued in more recent times, they nonetheless provide us with a starting point and, if you like, skeletal structures for exploring the ways in which children develop.

One such theorist who has explored the field of human development more generally is Abraham Maslow. Maslow (1970) was a humanist psychologist who offered a theory human motivation relating to human growth based on needs gratification. He suggested a hierarchy of human needs which, he maintained, correspond to the growth and maturity of the human person. When basic needs are met or gratified, such as physical needs – food, shelter, comfort, and the like – other higher and more complex needs would arise. He proposed the following five-level hierarchy of needs:

- Physiological needs: hunger, thirst
- Safety needs: need to be safe, free from pain, danger, anxiety
- Esteem: need for recognition by one's peers
- Belongingness and love: need for affection, to value and be valued as part of a group
- Self-actualization: need to develop one's potential, need to place long-term benefits to self and others before short term pleasures, develops a sense of priorities among needs, need to know "who am I?"

Activity 3.2: *In the story at the beginning of this chapter, which of David's developmental needs had been gratified?*

In terms of religious education, Maslow's hierarchy of needs has relevance. The second level particularly can be addressed in the early years' religious education classroom. The environment must be one in which children feel safe and free from anxiety if learning is to take place – not just in RE but in every curriculum area. The learning experiences which are planned and provided must avoid making the students feel anxious, afraid, and unsafe. This does not mean that the activities cannot be challenging for students. But rather that students are supported in their learning and have the opportunity of experiencing success in their efforts. This is essential if needs in the third level of esteem, and other consequent levels, are to be realized.

RELIGIOUS DEVELOPMENT: FOWLER'S STAGES OF FAITH DEVELOPMENT

Having been influenced by the structural-developmental psychologists such as Piaget and Kohlberg, theorist James Fowler researched the notion of faith and how faith might be understood to develop across the life span of a person. His work has been highly influential in the thinking of many religious educators, including those charged with the responsibility of planning syllabi in both primary and secondary contexts.

Fowler's (1981) understanding of faith varies from that of other theorists who have an interest in this area. For Fowler, faith is a human universal. It is something that all people have, for example, faith in a cause beyond themselves. It is concerned with more than belief in a particular religious tradition. Faith concerns the process of meaning making – a process in which all human beings engage. Fowler believes that this process of meaning making develops in predictable stages which are linked to chronological age. In drawing on the theories of structural – developmental psychology, Fowler maintains that each stage of faith broadly corresponds to the development in thinking capacities in people.

In his theory, Fowler describes seven stages of faith. Each of these is summarized briefly below:

Stage 1: Primal faith (Infancy)

In their infancy, children experience a primal faith gained from their interactions with their primary care-givers. Generally, it is an experience of trust which serves to offset the anxieties of separation that occur during the early childhood stages.

Stage 2: Intuitive-projective faith (early childhood)

This stage of faith development is most typical of early childhood. Children at this stage copy and reproduce the patterns of behavior of adults, especially their parents and care-givers. Children at this stage make meaning by intuition and by imitation. Fowler stresses the importance of imagination for the development of faith at this stage. Imagination can produce an array of images, many of which may be profound and which will last a lifetime. Fowler notes that young children in western countries are exposed to a wide range of images, both secular and religious, and that children will use these images to make meaning, including religious meaning. This can be so, even in instances where a child may have had no formal religious instruction or exposure to Church rituals.

Stage 3: Mythic-literal faith (childhood and beyond)

The most pertinent characteristic of this stage of faith development is the appropriating of the stories, beliefs and observances that symbolize affiliation with a particular group or community. Children at this stage also spend much time on sorting out reality from fantasy. While not ceasing to be imaginative, children begin to insist on proof of factual claims. Literal meanings become increasingly important at this stage. The child at this stage is also reliant on heroes and role models for shaping faith, and the authority of such role models will be implicitly accepted.

Stage 4: Synthetic-conventional faith (adolescence and beyond)

As the child approaches adolescence, their experience of the world begins to extend beyond their immediate family to take account of the wider world. Expanding interests now include school, perhaps work, peers, the media, and for some, religion. As a meaning-making activity, faith must now provide a coherence and synthesis of values and information which are now coming from a variety of sources. Fowler has suggested that although this stage is typical of adolescence, it becomes for many adults, the permanent reality.

Stage 5: Individuative-reflective faith (young adulthood and beyond)

This stage is not reached before late adolescence, if at all. It is characterized by the individual taking responsibility for her or his own lifestyle, commitments, beliefs and attitudes. People at this stage demonstrate the ability to be able to live with tensions or competing forces. A person at this stage can define her or himself in relation to a set of principle, such as justice, freedom and equality, rather than to a collection of significant others. This can render an individual politically or socially aware and committed to act on behalf of their guiding set of principles.

Stage 6: Conjunctive faith (early mid-life and beyond)

For those who attain this stage of faith development, there comes a need to come to terms with their own past and to rework it to find new meanings and multiple ways of meaning-making. This stage does not occur before mid-life, and even then, it is not common to find many people who attain it. Those who do are strongly committed to their own set of values, but at the same time, are able to be respectfully open to the views and truths of others. That is, they recognize that their own way of being does not encompass all other truths or ways of being.

Stage 7: Universalizing faith (mid-life and beyond)

The final stage of faith development is reached by very few people. Those who do attain this level no longer view themselves as individuals at the center of the universe. These people have instead put the ultimate at the center. They see that the core of all creation is a unity which resolves around all contradictions and conflicts. Boundaries between religion, gender and race disintegrate. Such people spend their time attempting to transform their present reality in the direction of that which is ultimate. Fowler identifies individuals such as Mother Teresa, Martin Luther King Jr and Mahatma Gandhi as those who may have attained this stage of faith development.

Activity 3.3: *Consider the first two stages of faith development, which are most pertinent to early childhood. What are some implications of these stages for religious education for early years classrooms?*

What characteristics of David and Emma, from the story at the beginning of this chapter may be indicative of their particular stage of faith according to Fowler's model?

A brief critique of Fowler

Fowler's stages of faith development theory has attracted both support and criticism. Ryan (2006) notes that those who have an interest in nurturing and fostering faith, such as religious educators, have praised Fowler's work for the insight it brings to the process of sharing faith. However, Fowler's concern is with *how* a person believes (the process) rather than *what* a person believes (the content). Thus, for those who criticize Fowler's model, it is difficult to distinguish between the faith of the religious believer, the atheist, and the humanist, since in Fowler's view, all have faith and are found at all stages. Others have argued that the influence of cognitive development in Fowler's model has rendered faith as a kind of knowing with little attention given to the role of feeling and values, which in fact are inextricably fused in faith.

SPIRITUAL DEVELOPMENT

The other area of human development in which there has been a growing concern, and in which religious education theorists are interested, is spiritual development. Since the word 'spirituality' has come to mean different things to different people, it is necessary to begin this section by briefly describing the meaning it has in this chapter.

Describing spirituality

What do we mean when we use the word 'spirituality'? Much of the contemporary research suggests that spirituality is concerned with a person's sense of connectedness or relationality with self, others, the world, and with a Transcendent dimension – God in the Christian tradition. Hay and Nye's (2006) study with children in Britain suggested that at the core of children's spirituality was what they have termed 'relational consciousness' – a conscious awareness of their sense of relationship with themselves and with everything other than themselves. Spirituality is a natural human predisposition. It is a quality that all human beings possess, regardless of whether or not they belong to, or practice, a particular religious tradition. Therefore, spirituality and religion are not the same thing, although a person's spirituality may be given expression through a religious tradition. So, regardless of a person's affiliation with religion, spirituality is expressed outwardly in terms of the relationships people have with the human and non-human world. Since spirituality is primarily concerned with the idea of relationship, and that could include a relationship with God, it is something that religious educators are particularly interested in, and something that they often seek to nurture through the classroom RE program.

Children's spirituality

There has been a growing body of research which attests to the spiritual dimension of children's lives. In the 1970s Edward Robinson's study at the Religious Experience Research unit at Oxford University discovered and reported on the recalled spiritual experiences from childhood by a large number of adults. Robinson (1977) asked the participants in his study to recall a time in their lives when they felt that their lives had been affected by some power beyond themselves. A significant number of these described profound experiences from childhood, which had remained vivid memories of the participants, and which held significance for them when contemplating questions relating to identity and meaning. While these accounts may have become embellished over time, Robinson argued that it was difficult to ignore the impact of these experiences, which in some way, generated reflection in the individual.

American child psychologist Robert Coles conducted a large scale study, in which he spoke directly to children aged between six and thirteen from a variety of countries to gain insight into the spiritual dimension of children's lives. In dialoging with these children, Coles (1990) placed an emphasis on listening attentively to the descriptions of these children's experiences and on their understandings of what they mean when they speak of God, thereby allowing the children to articulate for themselves their ultimate concerns. He found a rich tapestry of understanding in relation to children's spirituality, arguing that children do possess a spiritual dimension to their lives which can be accessed if adults listen attentively to them.

Since the work of these two scholars, others have sought to build upon their understandings, and to describe in more detail what is understood by children's spirituality. Such writers include Champagne (2003), Hart (2003), Eaude (2005), de Souza (2006) and Hyde (2008).

Spiritual development or spiritual integration?

While the research attests to the existence of a spiritual dimension to the lives of children, there is some question as to whether spirituality actually develops in children, at least in a Piagetian sense. That is, many theorists have questioned whether in fact children develop spiritually in the way that we think of them developing physically, or intellectually. In fact, Eaude (2005) and Priestley (2000) ague that children have qualities and features which are lost or suppressed as they get older. In some areas, such moral judgment, children develop. However, in others, such as the capacities for joy or curiosity, they seem to have something that adults loose. This may accord with how many religious traditions regard children as having access to a profound spirituality.

Hay and Nye (2006) suggest that, as children get older, their spirituality is suppressed or overlaid, by the processes of socialization that prevail in western culture. It is not common for people to discuss spiritual matters or express a sense of wonder and awe in relation to everyday occurrences. They tend to kept these private. As children grow older, they become socialized into a culture that relegates the spiritual to the private and often unacknowledged domain of the person. Hay and Nye argue that this discarding of spirituality is not a natural phenomenon. It is the task of religious educators to nurture and protect this dimension of children's lives. The role of the teacher becomes one of reconstructing a climate in which spirituality is nourished.

Rather than spiritual development, Eaude (2005) suggests the term could be envisioned as *spiritual integration*. The notion of integration implies that a person can regress as well as progress. If young children do possess important capacities such as openness, curiosity, and joy, the teacher must allow and enable these to flourish. In this way, spirituality is nurtured. Eaude (2005) and Hyde (2008) suggest that activities familiar to most classroom teachers can contribute to and nurture spirituality. That is, activities and learning experiences that already form a part of the curriculum, and in our case specifically, the classroom religious education program, may assist in nurturing the spirituality of children. The value of such activities is that they impact upon the growth and development in all aspects of their personality.

What might such activities look like? They would include opportunities for silence and solitude, as well as opportunities for interacting with others. They would include activities that arouse curiosity and activate a sense of wonder. They would also include learning experiences that enable children to develop a sense of empathy and compassion for others.

Characteristics of children's spirituality

So, what might children's spirituality look like? How might we, as educators, know when children are expressing their spirituality, and recognize it so that we can nurture it? Hyde (2008) identifies four particular features of children's spirituality – the felt sense, integrating awareness, weaving the threads of meaning, and spiritual questing.

The felt sense

As a characteristic of children's spirituality, the felt sense entails children attending to and being aware of their physical bodily awareness in relation to the activity or event in which they are engaged. When children encounter and act upon the world, they do so with the whole of their bodies. This includes both their physical and mental capacities. Bodily awareness is a primary source of knowing, although it is one which western culture conditions people to ignore in favor of intellectual detachment. Examples of activities which may lead to the felt sense could include running, skipping, painting, completing a jigsaw, using clay, and so forth. Such experiences can be holistic in that may engage the children's whole being.

Integrating awareness

Although somewhat complex, this characteristic occurs when a second level of awareness emerges and integrates previous levels of consciousness. In essence it involves the awareness of a physical activity, such as manipulating beads, or molding clay being integrated into an emerging level of awareness in a person, for example, when a person then speaks freely and intimately with a friend, or when a person is focused in prayer. The mystics of most religious traditions have been able to achieve this, and Hyde's (2008) study shows that children of primary school age too are able to integrate their awareness, albeit at much more basic levels, and for shorter periods of time.

Weaving the threads of meaning

Children's sense of wonder, Hyde (2008) discovered, acts as a tool for expressing their spirituality. He suggests that in wondering, children draw upon the many frameworks of meaning available to them – the media, their prior learning, their own experience, and the like – and choose eclectically from within these those elements that create meaning for themselves. They then weave these together into a personal framework of meaning. This can present a challenge for religious educators because often children select from frameworks of meaning which can be at odds with the Christian story, yet it is these very frameworks, Hyde argues, that ought to be the starting point for religiously educating children. That is, the Christian story needs to dialogue with the worldviews the children have woven together.

Spiritual questing

The children in Hyde's (2008) study were actively seeking authentic ways of connecting and of relating to self, others, the world, and to God. Spiritual questing is the term Hyde used to describe this characteristic of their spirituality. The children sought such a sense of connectedness through family, religion, acts of altruism, and through empathy with others. In some instances, they were also seeking a sense of connectedness through less traditional areas, such as astrology and the supernatural. Again, this highlights the importance of the Christian story dialoging with the reality of children's lives, and so may present some challenges for religious education.

CONCLUSION

In this chapter we have explored what some theorists have written in relation to the human, religious and spiritual development of young children. It is a broad field, and one which is continuing to grow, especially in relation to spirituality and young children. The implications for religious education in early years' classrooms are both numerous and complex. They require that religious educators take account of these when planning their classroom programs and courses of study.

FURTHER QUESTIONS AND ACTIVITIES

1. Read again the story of David and Emma at the beginning of this chapter. Which elements are indicative of their human, religious and spiritual development respectively?

2. What do you think about Eaude's (2005) suggestion that children may not develop spiritually, at least, not in a Piagetian sense? Discuss your response with a partner.

3. Examine the four characteristics of children's spirituality identified by Hyde (2008). Can you think of times when you may have seen examples of each characteristic in young children?

4. What are the implications for religious education for each of Hyde's identified characteristics of children's spirituality?

5. Under three headings, list the implications for religious education when considering the human, religious and spiritual development of children in early years classrooms.

REFERENCES

Coles, R. (1990). *The spiritual life of children*. London: HarperCollins.

Champagne, E. (2003). Being a child, a spiritual child. *International Journal of Children's Spirituality*, 8 (1), 43-53.

de Souza, M. (2006). Rediscovering the spiritual dimension in education: Promoting a sense of self and place, meaning and purpose in learning. In M. de Souza *et al.* (Eds.), *International handbook of the religious, moral and spiritual dimensions in education* (pp. 1127-1139). Dordrecht, The Netherlands: Springer.

Eaude, T. (2005). Strangely familiar? – Teachers making sense of young children's spiritual development. *Early Years, 25* (3), 237-248.

Fowler, J. (1981). *Stages of faith: The psychology of human development and the quest for meaning.* Blackburn, VIC: CollinsDove.

Hart, T. (2003). *The secret spiritual world of children.* Makawao, HI: Inner Ocean.

Hay, D., & Nye, R. (2006). *The spirit of the child* (rev. ed). London: Jessica Kingsley.

Hyde, B. (2008). *Children and spirituality: Searching for meaning and connectedness.* London: Jessica Kingsley.

Maslow, A. (1970). *Motivation and personality* (2nd ed.). New York: Harper & Row.

Priestley, J. (2000). Moral and spiritual growth. In J. Mills & R. Mills (Eds.), *Childhood studies: A reader in perspectives of childhood* (pp. 113-128). London: Routledge.

Robinson, E. (1977). *The original vision: A study of the religious experience of childhood.* Manchester College, Oxford: The Religious Experience Research Unit.

Ryan, M. (2006). *Religious education in Catholic schools: An introduction for Australian students.* Melbourne, VIC: David Lovell.

CHAPTER 4

PEDAGOGICAL INFLUENCES ON EARLY YEARS' RELIGIOUS EDUCATION CLASSROOMS

A scenario:

Susan is an early years' classroom teacher. In religious education, her class is exploring the topic of "Holy Week". The children are engaged in a number of different activities associated with this topic. Susan is working with one group of children. She is helping them to create a wall chart with key terms that are used during Holy Week, such as "Palm Sunday", "Holy Thursday", and "Good Friday". She is "scaffolding" the learning through providing a series of pictures and illustrations of these events, by using the language which the Tradition of the Church attributes to these events, and by encouraging the students to engage in this language. Another group is in the dress-up corner. They are about to role play Jesus entering Jerusalem. There is also a group of children working with small milk cartons. These children are trying to create the Temple in Jerusalem, using a large digital image which Susan has given them. A fourth group of children is in the home-corner, which has been set up to depict the Last Supper. These children are examining and labeling some of the table items – goblet, unleavened bread, and so forth.

Question

What do you notice about the types of activities that Susan has planned for the students in the above scenario? Discuss your response with a partner.

There has been considerable discussion and development in recent years in relation to contemporary early childhood theory and practice. It is imperative that religious education pedagogy in early years' settings is informed by such advancement. To ignore the breadth of research in this field would be to risk the development of a pedagogical model that would contradict effective early childhood practice.

In this chapter we explore three particular approaches that have emanated from the field of early childhood theory and practice, and how these might impact upon effective pedagogy in early years' classrooms. While it is acknowledged that there are other approaches, those detailed in this chapter have been included because their application to religious education in early years' settings can be clearly seen. The three approaches that will be investigated are:

- The constructivist approach;
- Play-based learning, and
- Developmentally Appropriate Practice

THE CONSTRUCTIVIST APPROACH

In essence, a constructivist approach views learning as an active process in which the learner constructs knowledge. This is in contrast to some traditional teacher-centered methodologies in which the educator imparts knowledge and the students are viewed as passive learners. In a constructivist model of learning, children are engaged in tasks which are designed to create personal meaning. Some psychologists, such as Jean Piaget, argued that children construct their own understanding through interaction with their environment. This is known as *personal constructivism*. Piaget in particular argued that intellectual development occurred through a series of stages which were characterized by qualitatively discrete cognitive structures. This is often referred to as *structuralism*. Piaget's believed that in each of these stages of development there is a characteristic way in which children think about the world and solve problems. At each stage, children develop increasingly more sophisticated metal processes, leading eventually to the acquisition of fully logical cognitive operations (McInerney & McInerney, 2006).

However, others such as Lev Vygotsky argued for a cultural-historical theory, in which learning is viewed as a process of appropriation by the child of culturally relevant behaviors. As a key figure in the development of such an approach, Vygotsky argued that learning is not a passive, solitary undertaking, but rather that it is a socially constructed activity. In other words, he placed importance upon the role of the child's social and cultural world in their construction of meaning (McInerney & McInerney, 2006). According to Vygotsky's theory, children are born with a wide range of perceptual, attitudinal and memory capabilities which are substantially transformed in the context of socialization and education, particularly through inventions such as "tools", social structure and language, to constitute the higher psychological functions or the unique forms of human cognition. Such "tools" could consist of pens, paintbrushes, calculators, and other various symbol systems, including language and mathematical notation. Of importance also in Vygotsky's theory are the social structures and language systems of the learner. Learning develops then as a process through which the individual becomes one with the collective through carrying out personal activity in collaboration with others. For Vygotsky, cognitive development is not so much the expansion of mental schemes within the individual (as in Piagetian theory), but rather the unfolding of cognitive understandings of social beings within social contexts. The individual becomes a part of the community, and the community becomes part of the individual in the sharing of knowledge (McInerney & McInerney, 2006).

The social nature of learning is indeed a feature of many early years' classrooms, where children work with others in small groups, and where interaction with other children is both valued and encouraged. Some writers have suggested that constructivist classrooms may be more effective in encouraging children's cognitive, social and moral development than are classrooms which employ more teacher-centered models (Gordon & Williams-Browne, 2000).

In constructivist models of learning procedural knowledge – characterized by trial and error, copying by doing, and the like – is favored over factual knowledge. Such activities characteristic of procedural knowledge would engage students in their learning, and might involve tasks such as writing, devising, making, presenting, or even interviewing, rather than simply completing a series of questions on an activity sheet (Chase, 2000).

This type of learning has a definite place in the early years' religious education classroom. For example, Grajczonek (2004) notes that, in a constructivist model of learning, students might be "baptizing" a doll in the focus corner, or reconstructing the Temple in Jerusalem with blocks or other materials after hearing the story about Jesus being lost there. Grajczonek argues that in this type of learning the student is engaged with the subject matter in more concrete and involved ways than are students who can answer question such as: "What are the symbols of the sacrament of Baptism?" or "Where did Mary and Joseph find Jesus when he was lost?"

The notion of scaffolding is an important aspect of the social constructivist approach. The socio-cultural theory advanced by Vygotsky placed significance upon the role of adults who provide support for children as they move to a higher level of performance in what he termed the "zone of proximal development" (ZPD) (Williams, 1999). ZPD is a complex and somewhat debated concept. In essence it refers to each person's range of potential for learning. Vygotsky describes the ZPD as the distance between the actual developmental level of the child and the level of potential development as determined through problem solving under the guidance of adults or in collaboration with more capable peers (McInerney and McInerney, 2006). To situate learning in the ZPD, an appropriate level of difficulty needs to be established. This must be challenging, but not too difficult. The educator then needs to provide guided practice to the child with a definite sense of the intended goal or outcome of the child's performance. This is referred to as "scaffolded instruction". As with scaffolding around a building, it is gradually removed so that, in time, the child can perform the task independently. If the learning experience has been carefully structured and situated within the child's ZPD, the child should, in time, be able to master the skill, or perform the task independently.

Some scholars, such as Gallimore and Tharp (1990) have noted that there are four stages through which a child progresses in the ZPD. These are detailed blow:

1. Assistance: In this initial stage, the performance is assisted by those more capable, such parents, teachers, and perhaps peers.

2. Growing independence: Here, there is less dependence and performance begins to become personalized. Children begin to help themselves and begin to take responsibility for self-guidance.

3. Automation of response: Performance is developed, automated and internalized.

4. De-automatization and recursion: In this final stage, if the new knowledge or skill has not been used, a de-automatization may occur which leads the individual to re- enter the ZPD. For example, sometimes even well learned responses are forgotten or become rusty. In this sense, there may be, for some, a continual movement in and out of the ZPD. Gallimore and Tharp (1990) refer to this as 'recursion'.

Scaffolding has a crucial role to play in religious education, where children's religious knowledge and understanding can be limited. The notion of scaffolding is more than simply being able to help children solve problems. It involves providing the appropriate resources and materials to support children in their learning. For example, Grajczonek (2004) notes that in religious education, scaffolding might include providing vivid images of the Temple in Jerusalem, or of people wearing the clothes of Jesus' time. Such images would help children to visualize and imagine what life might have been like and how Jesus may have become lost in a large building like the Temple which had so many different sections and rooms. Scaffolding requires the religious educator to be aware of the children's needs in terms of concepts, language and experience. It involves being "in tune with [children's] thinking and being ready to step in at opportune times to supply that missing piece of information…or to ask the right question that guides children to further learning without taking over" (Grajczonek, 2004, p. 54).

While the social-constructivist approach is appropriate for early years' classrooms, it nonetheless presents some challenges for religious educators. Many children do not experience religion as a natural part of their childhood experience, and so many teachers may feel the need to shift their teaching from a child-centered pedagogy to one that is more teacher-directed. However, this need not be the case, as religious education could be a negotiated curriculum in which students are supported to construct their own learning. For example, after visiting the Church for a school celebration, students could construct models of the Church. The various pieces of furniture and icons could be discussed and labeled, perhaps even made using plasticene and other materials. Small figures could be used to represent the priest and other members of the celebration. The young children could then be involved in "playing" with the constructions, thereby making meaning and understanding of the event. There would be much rich language generated from this type of activity that could then form the basis of student's own re-telling, perhaps in the form of a big book, or slide-show using a computer program such as KidsPix.

However, all of this would need to involve careful planning on the part of the early years' educator. Because religion is not a part of many children's lives, and they therefore do not have a natural starting point for constructing their own knowledge in this area, teachers may have to initiate the learning and balance appropriately the need for teacher-centered learning with child-centered learning.

PLAY-BASED LEARNING

As it is now widely accepted that children learn through play, the place of play in early childhood education is universally recognized. Through play, children develop their imaginations, as well as practice language and relationship skills. It is a means by which they are able to make sense of their experiences. It may provide them with opportunities to go beyond the ordinary, and to discover for themselves the meanings and values of their experiences (Bredekamp, 1988; Kostelnick, 1992; Ure, 1993).

The notion of sociodramatic play, or pretend play, is a key feature of young children in early years' settings, and can consist of both elements of make-believe and reality-based play. Bretherton (cited in Hymans, 1996) describes pretend play as consisting of two levels. The first level – make-believe play – pertains to the "as if" dimension, in which children are involved in familiar situations, such as shopping, or having a party. In this type of play, children actually shop or play party games as if they were actually involved in the real event itself. The second level comprises the "what if" dimension. In this level, children transform the real world into a fictional, or fantasy world, in which a spoon or block of wood becomes the telephone, and in which children pretend to be mothers and fathers, doctors and nurses.

The religious education program in early years' classrooms can reflect the above ideas in practice. Just as teachers set up the home corner of their classroom to become, for example, the supermarket checkout, or the post office, where both "as if" and "what if" dimensions of play can take place, so it can also be set up as, for example, the baptismal area in the Church. A doll's bath tub, a white garment, some candle sticks, and other items could be set up there for children to utilize and play with. These items can named, and the language written into labels – "Baptismal font", "white garment", Easter candle" – and displayed in the home corner. As the children role-play the baptism, they would be then using new terminology, and experience the opportunity of using this new language in non-threatening ways. This could be followed by a visit to the Church, where an exploration of the baptismal area could reinforce the language explored in the classroom and the home corner. In this particular example, the classroom teacher would also be using the language associated with Baptism, and hopefully, joining in the role-playing of the children, thereby effectively modeling how to use the specific language of Baptism.

Grajczonek (2004) notes that for young children, learning to use religious language is often like learning a second language. Therefore, they need to be provided with opportunities for play which may in turn provide a safe space for children to practice using their new language.

Play-based learning can provide children in early years' classrooms with opportunities for actively investigating, questioning, practicing and clarifying many aspects within the religious education program. It enables children to experiment and to take risks with new language and concepts in a non-threatening manner. Play-based learning is an approach that can and should be drawn upon by teachers in early years' classrooms.

DEVELOPMENTALLY APPROPRIATE PRACTICE

As discussed Jean Paiget is another theorist who has been influential in the area of early childhood development, and it is Piagetian theory that underpins the notion of Developmentally Appropriate Practice (DAP) which emanates from the United States of America. DAP draws on three pivotal and interrelated bodies of knowledge: (1) what is known by educators about how children develop and learn; (2) what is known by teachers about each of the individual children in their group; and (3) what is known about the social and cultural contexts in which those children live and learn.

Grajczonek (2004) notes that DAP has attracted its fair share of criticism from early childhood specialists for many reasons, including the limitations of Piagetian theory, as well as for its lack of consideration of the role that children's social contexts have upon their learning. Despite these criticism, there are some aspects of DAP that are worthy of consideration by religious educators in early years' classrooms. For instance, DAP regards all domains of development – physical, social, emotional and cognitive – as being interrelated. Therefore, development in one domain effects and is affected by development in each of the other domains. Further, if the focus of development remains in one domain only, for example, the cognitive domain, then the other areas are violated. A clear implication here is that learning in early years' religious education needs to go beyond the cognitive dimension. It is not enough to have young children listen to Bible stories or to be told how they should act like Jesus. Children need to be active in their learning. They need to be engaged learners. For example, rather than just being told stories from the Bible, children in early years' religious education classrooms could dress up as the Biblical characters with materials from the dress-up corner that reflect the clothes of that period of time. Instead of drawing pictures of the items found in the Church, children in early years' religious education classrooms need to visit and tour the Church regularly, and to role-play back in the classroom using the models of the vessels that are used on the altar – the chalice, the ciborium, candles, and so forth. Such activities help to engage and develop other domains beyond the cognitive. Chapter 10 also addresses some ways in which this might be achieved by considering the affective and spiritual dimensions as well as the cognitive.

Another challenge which DAP raises concerns the notion of the integrated curriculum. It argues that when confronted with information, the human brain seeks to make meaningful connections with what is already known. Young children engaging with religious education for the first time are presented an array of new information for which, because religion for most is not a part of their life experience, they have little or no previous knowledge with which to connect it. It becomes difficult for them to make sense of learning in this new area.

Teachers of children in early years' classrooms need to be aware of this, and provide children with experiences in which they can engage with religious knowledge, new language and concepts, practice using them and take risks with them. However, this does not mean that teachers should "dumb-down" the religious education program. Precisely because of the above challenges, children will require opportunities to explore deeply and to attend in great detail to religious education as a subject area.

Related to the above is the DAP assertion that young children develop their vocabulary in relation to a particular topic by being provided with explicit opportunities to talk about a particular topic. Teachers of early years' classrooms then need to listen attentively to children so that they can offer expansions to the sentences of children to enhance meaning. Grajczonek (2004) notes that this is challenging for both teachers and children in their first year of schooling, since many children do not have a starting point for talking about religion. Children who have little or no experience of a religious tradition find it difficult to initiate a conversation about it. It will be up to the teacher to initiate this conversation without manipulating the children. Strategies used in other subject areas may be useful here – wall charts, posters, dramatic play and other experiences requiring communication and informal chat could be utilized. Providing a print-rich environment is helpful, but such environments do not just happen. They require the forethought and planning of the perceptive religious educator.

CONCLUSION

The three approaches outlined in this chapter – the constructivist approach (and in particular, the social constructivist approach), play-based learning and developmentally appropriate practice – emanate from the field of early childhood theory and practice and provide challenges to teaching religious education in early years' classrooms. These approaches are not definitive. No one of these approaches can be considered as the most appropriate. Each has insights to offer, and as in any other educational sector, early childhood education consists largely of a combination of these, and other, approaches, implemented in various ways. However, the implications of these approaches for religious education in early years' settings must be carefully and critically considered.

FURTHER QUESTIONS AND ACTIVITIES

1. Design a T-Chart comparing the similarities and differences of each of the approaches discussed in this chapter.

2. What type of scaffolding activities and experiences might you consider in planning a unit of work focusing on "The Eucharist"?

3. Imagine you are planning a unit of work on "The Church" for children in an early years' classroom. Based on the approaches discussed in this chapter, list four activities that you would include in your learning and teaching for the students.

4. Can you think of any religious education topic in which feel that you could not draw on one of the approaches outlined in this chapter. Discuss and justify your response with a partner.

5. How might you as the teacher initiate a conversation with young children on Pentecost? List three ways in which you might do this (some of the suggestions under the Developmentally Appropriate Practice section of this chapter might be helpful).

REFERENCES

Bredekamp, S. (1998). NAEYC position statement on developmentally appropriate practice in primary grades, serving 5-through 8-year olds. *Young Children, 43* (2), 64-84.

Chase, L. (2000). Language development. In D. Nixon & K. Gould (Eds.), *Extending child development from five to twelve years* (pp. 79-99). Katoomba, NSW: Social Science Press.

Gallimore, R., & Tharp, R. (1990). Teaching mind in society: Teaching, schooling and literate discourse. In L.C.Moll (Ed.), *Vygotsky and education*. New York: Cambridge.

Gordon, A., & Williams-Browne, K. (2000). *Beginnings and beyond* (5th ed.). Australia: Delmar Thomson Learning.

Grajczonek, J. (2004). Stop, look and learn: Re-visioning pedagogy in early years' religion settings. *Journal of Religious Education, 52* (3), 52-59.

Hymans, D. (1996). Let's play: The contribution of the pretend play of children to religious education in a pluralist context. *Religious Education, 91* (3), 368-381.

Kostelnick, M. (1992). Myths associated with developmentally appropriate programs. *Young Children*, May, 17-23.

McInerney, D., & McInerney, V. (2006). *Educational psychology: Constructing learning* (4th ed). Frenchs Forest, NSW: Pearson Prentice Hall.

Ure, C. (1993). The early years of schooling: More on a developmental learning perspective. *Curriculum Exchange 12* (2), 11.

Williams, L. (1999). Determining the early years childhood curriculum: The evolution of goals and strategies through consonance and controversy. In C. Seefeld (Ed.), *The early childhood curriculum: Current findings in theory and practice* (3rd ed.). New York: Teachers College Press.

CHAPTER 5

GODLY PLAY – A WAY OF RELIGIOUS EDUCATION FOR EARLY YEARS' SETTINGS

> I can't make you play, because play doesn't work that way.
> An essential quality of play is its freedom: its lack of compulsion.
> Do you want to play? Berryman (2002, p. 11)

There are many different approaches to religious education in early years' settings. While almost all of them draw upon what is known about child development, they differ in their method according to whether the purpose of the program is catechetical (aimed at inviting children into relationship with God), or educational (learning about religion). Some programs are educational with catechetical intent.

In this chapter we will explore an approach to religious education for young children known as Godly Play. It has its origins in an approach used for Sunday school teaching, and so is catechetical. However, it has been adapted and drawn upon in the religious education curriculum of primary schools in dioceses around the world, including Australia (Hyde, 2004, 2007). It is an innovative approach which has much to offer early years classrooms, and so is worthy of exploration.

WHAT IS GODLY PLAY?

What is Godly Play? In essence, Godly Play is not play in general; it is play with the language of God and God's people: the sacred stories, parables, liturgical actions and silences. Through this powerful language, through wondering, through the community of players gathered together, the deepest invitation of all is offered – an invitation to come to play with God.

So, how did Godly Play come about?

During the 1970's, an American Episcopalian vicar named Jerome Berryman studied at The Centre for Advanced Montessori Studies in Bergamo, Italy. Maria Montessori, upon whom the centre was founded, had developed an approach to education which, in essence, rested on two foundational premises – to educate the senses, and to educate the intellect. A child's interaction with a carefully prepared learning environment was found to achieve these aims. Montessori (1963) had also stressed the power of the child in her or his ability to understand even the most complicated of concepts. She had argued that educators must recognize the ability of children to do this, and to discern ways in which to nurture it.

While studying at The Centre for Advanced Montessori Studies, Berryman was introduced to the work of Sofia Cavalletti, a renowned Hebrew Scripture scholar, and her colleagues. They had developed a process for catechesis with young children. Known as *The Catechesis of the Good Shepherd*, the process was grounded in scriptural and liturgical study framed by Montessori's principles of education. This allowed children to hear the Gospel through the use of sensorial rich materials. These included three dimensional objects such as dolls, figurines, and the like which could be physically handled and manipulated. The children were free to work with these materials that represented essential proclamations of the Christian message. *The Catechesis of the Good Shepherd* thus brought together a unique combination of biblical scholarship and early childhood education. Cavalletti and her colleagues had observed that young children possess a special capacity to experience the presence of the God who is already present to them in the inner-most depths of their being. They found this to be so, even in instances where the child had no explicit religious upbringing (Cavalletti, 1983).

Today the *Catechesis of the Good Shepherd* can be found in many liturgical traditions (Episcopalian, Lutheran, and Roman Catholic) as well as in schools throughout the world. It has grown and spread amazingly to at least 19 countries – Argentina, Bolivia, Brazil, Canada, Chile, Colombia, Croatia, Ireland, Italy, Japan, Mexico, New Zealand, Panama, Singapore, Tanzania, and the United States.

Upon his return to the United States of America, and having been influenced by Cavalletti's work, Berryman embarked upon his own project, carrying forward the work of Cavalletti. He developed a process for Sunday school catechesis which he called Godly Play. Berryman describes Godly Play as his interpretation of Montessori religious education. The idea of play is central to the process. Play is the way in which children learn to do things, from the use of language to opening and closing doors. Play is the child's 'work'. Through play, children develop their imagination and relationships with others. It may provide them with opportunities to transcend – to go beyond the ordinary, and to discover for themselves the meaning and value of their own experiences (Healy, Hyde & Rymarz, 2004).

However, Berryman's (2002) understanding of play is a little more specific than what is described above. He uses a five-part description to explain what he understands by play:

1. Play is pleasurable, enjoyable;
2. Play has no extrinsic goals. It is played for itself;
3. Play is spontaneous and voluntary. It is freely chosen by the player;
4. Play involves deep and active engagement on the part of the players;
5. Play has systematic relations to what is not play such as creativity, problem solving, language learning, the development of social roles and other cognitive and social phenomena.

In other words, there has to be an *invitation* to play, not a directive based on power. For a person to enter Godly Play, they must find it enjoyable, and want to play it for its own sake. A person must choose to play it because she or he wants to play the game.

THE GOALS AND OBJECTIVES OF GODLY PLAY

The goal of Godly Play is essentially to teach young children the art of using the language of the Christian tradition as a means by which to encounter God and to find direction for their lives. Berryman (1995) outlines six particular objectives that help to achieve this goal.

1. To model how to wonder in religious education, so children can "enter" religious language, rather than merely repeating it or talking about it.
2. To show children how to create meaning with the language of the Christian tradition and how this can involve them in the experience of the Creator.
3. To show children how to choose their own work, so they can confront their own existential limits and depth issues rather than work on other kinds of problems dictated by others, including adults.
4. To organize the educational time to follow the pattern of worship that the Christian tradition has found to be the best way to be with God in community.
5. To show children how to work together as a community by supporting and respecting each other and one another's quest.
6. To organize the educational space so that the whole system of Christian language is present in the room, so children can literally walk into that language domain when they enter the room and can begin to make connections among its various parts as they work with the lesson of the day and their responses in art or other lessons.

OUTLINE OF THE PROCESS

An initial consideration: The prepared environment

In outlining the process of Godly Play, the first thing to note is the importance of the prepared environment. The environment in which children work and play was seen by Montessori as critical in meeting their educational needs. For example, children from the ages of three to six require furnishings appropriate to their physical size. They need to be able to locate and collect materials for themselves from shelving at their own height.

The environment also needs to be maintained and cared for. And, in drawing upon these principles, Berryman argues that it also needs to be well prepared. In a Godly Play classroom, the furniture will be carefully arranged. There will be different shelves containing various aids for the lesson – a shelf for Parables of the Church, an Easter Self, Sacred Story shelves containing stories from the Hebrew (Old) and Christian (New) Testaments. As well, there will be a focus shelf, and a shelf containing children's 'work-in-progress'. There will be spaces set aside for listening, spaces for playing, and spaces for quiet.

There are six essential elements which comprise Godly Play. Each of these is detailed and explored below.

1 Crossing the threshold (entering)

In Berryman's process, the threshold is important. It is the invitation to enter a new space. The Godly Play classroom door acts in this way. It divides the language and action of the everyday world from the language and action of the Christian people, which is clarified and expressed inside the Christian education classroom.

The significance of thresholds is often marked in church buildings by the front steps, the special carvings above the entrance, and the like. When people enter, they move from the ordinary world into a new space. The doorway marks the place where one begins to 'get ready' to enter this new space

At the doorway to the Godly Play classroom is positioned an adult who has the role of the Doorperson. The key role of the

Doorperson is to welcome and greet each child by name as they arrive. In this way, the doorperson helps each child enter the new space by crossing the threshold. The greeting, the friendly smile, and even a quick chat with the child's parents establish the Godly Play classroom as a welcoming space, and one which the child wants to enter.

2 The circle and presentation

The children, sitting in a circle, formally begin the lesson. Circles, as Berryman reminds us, are fundamental symbols. Circles never end. The seasons of nature circle around us. The life sequences of many animals – tadpole/frogs, caterpillars/butterflies, water bugs/dragon flies are depicted as circular, that is, a life cycle.

Just as indigenous peoples from all cultures sit in circles to remember and to tell stories, in the Sunday school setting, Berryman argues, we too sit in a circle with children. We invoke the ancient memories of the faith tradition through the stories of the tradition, and so the themes of scripture become present to us today.

In the centre of the circle are placed the materials that will be used to tell the story. Usually, the story comes from scripture. But it can also come from liturgical action. The materials may include three-dimensional figurines, finger puppets, a felt board, and other small artifacts. These materials are used to literally tell the story. Most often, the teacher, or storyteller is Berryman's terms, will initially manipulate these materials during the story telling, but often, children will be invited to maneuver them. This will certainly happen later in the process.

3 Group wondering

After the story has been told the teacher, or storyteller, guides and supports what is known as "group wondering". This is not a question-and-answer time. There are no set answers. Helping the children to wonder about the story which has been presented guides them in learning how to use religious language. This wondering includes the teacher! In fact, it is essential that the teacher wonders with the children.

Berryman describes the interaction that takes place between the teacher and children in wondering as "seriously playful". It is serious because it guides the children in the use of religious language, which they can use to cope with their own "existential limits" (we will return to this term in a moment). But it is playful because children learn what attracts and interest them, and helps them grow. The teacher's involvement in this wondering is critical:

> When the teacher is truly wondering, the children sense wonder in the air. It manifests itself in the playfulness present in the room. Permission and reinforcement are present to encourage it. When the teacher enters religious language with wonder, he or she shows the children by example how to open the creative process. (Berryman, 1991, p. 62)

There are different types of wondering for the different kinds of religious language evoked by the story. For instance, with parables, which provoke the un-thinkable, the wondering could include "I wonder what this could really be?" In the parable of the mustard seed, the storyteller might ask, "I wonder if the birds have names? I wonder how the birds found their way to the great tree?"

If the story is a sacred story (stories that shape identity, such as the Creation story), the storyteller might ask, "I wonder what part of the story you like best? I wonder what part of the story is most important? I wonder if there is any part of the story we can leave out and still have the story?"

If the story is related to liturgical action and symbol (such as Lent, Baptism), the storyteller might ask, "I wonder which of these great times you like best? I wonder how the colors make you feel? I wonder why we use water?" Sometimes, even, "Hmm, I wonder…" may be enough to evoke a sense of wonder…a sense of the sacred.

4 Response

When the wondering has concluded, the storyteller invites each child to go and take out her or his own work. Their "work" is usually in direct response to the story and the wondering which have just taken place. The shelves where the various items of equipment are stored (art supply shelves, Easter shelf, parables shelf, etc). In keeping the Montessorian principles, they are intentionally set up to provide children with open access to whatever they need in order to express themselves. Some children may wish to retell the story again by manipulating the three dimensional materials. Some may which to draw or to paint. Some may wish to use clay as a medium through which to respond to the story. If the Liturgical action of Baptism formed the basis of the presentation, some children may wish to use water to "baptize their own baby", role-playing the various parts of the presider, the parents, godparents, etc. It is here particularly that the environment needs to be carefully prepared.

5. The Feast

In following the pattern of the Eucharistic celebration, the feast follows the response. Children are invited to put away their work and help prepare for the feast. In the Godly Play classroom, the Doorperson, working with two or three children prepare the feast while the others return to the circle. Items for the feast usually include a basket with napkins, a tray with biscuits, and a tray with cordial already poured into cups. This is an indirect form of preparation for their eventual participation in Holy Communion.

6. Leaving

After sharing in the feast, everything is put away, and the children prepare to leave. Again, the Doorperson has a pivotal role to play here. The Doorperson acknowledges and greets the parents as they arrive to collect children. And, the Doorperson personally says "Good bye" by naming each child individually as they once again go through the threshold.

Other principles

Religious language and existential limits

An important part of the Godly Play process is learning to acquire religious language so that children can transcend the existential limits to their lives. What is meant by existential limits? Berryman (1995) says they are parts of life which include our need for meaning, our personal death, the threat of freedom, and our fundamental aloneness. They are the boundaries that mark us as human beings. They define our existence.

These existential limits are just as fundamental to the lives of children as they are to adults. While children may experience and speak of them in ways different to adults, they are nonetheless real for them. Providing opportunities for children to acquire and use religious language in order to find meaning and so to transcend these existential limits fundamental to the Godly Play process. The group wondering in particular provides an opportunity for children to explore and use such language "playfully" and in a way that is supported by the teacher.

Kairos and chronos time

In a Godly Play setting, time is managed so that the children who enter the room enter into *kairos* time – a time that is both orderly and leisurely. No one will rush them. The teacher will tell the children that they have all the time they need. *Kairos* time is not concerned with knowing what the time is. This is the role of *chronos* time, or chronological, clock time. Rather the *kairos* time involved in Godly Play allows time for both the children and the teacher time to see God in the centre of daily life and to reflect on what time is for. Berryman (2002) reminds us that this kind of orderly and leisurely time is the gift that the mystics throughout history have given themselves to experience their own playful prayer with God. *Kairos* time is *significant* time.

CONCLUSION

What has been presented in this chapter is certainly not exhaustive, but provides an introduction to the Godly Play process as one way of religious education for children in early years settings. The references listed at the end of this chapter may provide you with additional insight. As Berryman presents it, the Godly Play process is not entirely suitable for the primary school classroom. This is because it was designed for a Sunday school setting which parallels closely the pattern of Christian worship. The primary school classroom does not share this aim. However, the principles that underlie the process are valuable and are certainly worth consideration. The religious education curricula for early years classrooms of major dioceses in several countries, particularly Australia, have been influenced by the Godly Play approach. Notable among these, is the *To know, worship and love* series (Elliott, 2005) which is used in the Catholic Archdiocese of Melbourne and Sydney, and which is drawn on elsewhere.

FURTHER QUESTIONS AND ACTIVITIES

1. Have you heard of Godly Play? Use the internet to source web sites in relation to this process for religious education. What do these sites have to say?

2. Have you seen this approach, or one that seems similar to it, used in classrooms on your practicum?

3. Examine the six objectives that Berryman outlines for Godly Play. Discuss the implications of these for early years' classrooms.

4. In small groups, discuss the notion of existential limits. What might these mean for young children? Have you seen evidence of them impacting upon young children?

5. Suppose you were developing a unit of work on "Creation". What are some possible group wondering questions you might draw upon? Record these and compare them with a partner.

6. What are some possible response activities you might include for a presentation centered on the theme "Pentecost"?

REFERENCES

Berryman, J. (1991). *Godly play: A way of religious education.* San Francisco: Harper.

Berryman, J. (1995). *Teaching Godly play: The Sunday morning handbook.* Nashville: Abingdon.

Berryman, J. (2002). *The complete guide to Godly Play. Volume 1.* Denver, Colorado: Living the Good News.

Cavalletti, S. (1983). *The religious potential of the child: The description of an experience with children from ages three to six.* New York: Paulist Press.

Elliott, P. (Gen Ed.). (2005). *To know, worship and love series, level 1 and 2.* Melbourne: James Goold House Publications.

Healy, H., Hyde, B., & Rymarz, R. (2004). *Making our way through primary RE: A handbook for religious educators.* Tuggerah, NSW: Social Science Press.

Hyde, B. (2004). Children's spirituality and "The Good Shepherd Experience". *Religious Education, 99* (2), 137-150.

Hyde, B. (2007). The catechesis of the Good Shepherd: A Case Study. In J. Grajczonek, & M. Ryan (Eds.), *Religious education in early childhood: A reader* (pp. 103-115). Brisbane: Lumino Press.

Montessori, M. (1063). *Education for a new world.* India: Kalakshetra Publications. (Original work published 1946).

CHAPTER 6

PLANNING FOR RE: LOOKING AT CURRICULUM FRAMEWORKS

The Religious Education (RE) curriculum in Catholic schools in Australia is set by Catholic Education Offices (CEOs) situated in each diocese. Australia does not have a national or even statewide RE curriculum. The curriculum is developed by the CEO in collaboration with schools and other educational groups and then approved by the local bishop. This system has parallels with other countries such as Canada which also lack a national RE curriculum program. Some provinces, such as Alberta, also lack a provincial-wide curriculum.

Most RE curricula are based on some type of conceptual framework or model that seeks to identify the key influences that have shaped the curriculum. The Archdiocese of Melbourne has nominated five key areas that are pivotal in shaping classroom RE. They are:

> 1. The Scriptures and the message of Jesus Christ and openness to their significance for living.
> 2. The living Tradition of the Catholic Church and a willingness to participate in its mission.
> 3. God and creation, awareness of existence of good and evil, and a capacity to search effectively for meaning in life.
> 4. God in prayer, liturgy and the sacraments and a willingness to participate in both personal and communal prayer.
> 5. Catholic moral teaching and an ability to work for justice in the world

Activity 6.1: *Research curriculum documents from other dioceses. Come up with another model that is used to describe the influences on the RE curriculum.*

One aspect of the educational approach to religious education is the importance that is given to planning a rigorous and robust curriculum. As with other aspects of the curriculum the educational approach stresses the overlap between what is done in religious education and what is done in other areas of the school's curriculum. If this is the case then there should not be a wide disparity for how teaching and learning is situated in religious education when compared with other subject disciplines. The content of an RE program should be a rich and varied content that comprehensively covers a range of areas that make up religious education. One influential way of developing a content model of religious education is to follow a typological approach. This breaks up the curriculum content into a number of key content areas such as Scripture, sacrament, moral teaching and others. With typological models the number of types can vary, and so can the number of times topics are repeated in the curriculum. In a thorough content model key topics such as Eucharist should be repeated a number of times, with increasing complexity, over the years. As students get older their understanding of concepts should become more sophisticated, and one way of ensuring this is to revisit topics in a new and more challenging way. This is am example of the spiral curriculum.

DIOCESAN RELIGIOUS EDUCATION DOCUMENTS

Below is part of the content overview for the primary religious education curriculum used in Catholic primary schools in the Archdiocese of Sydney. Obtained from http://ceo.syd.catholic.edu.au/cms/webdav/site/reonline/shared/Religious%20education/Primary/Curriculum

Kindergarten	Year 1	Year 2
K.1 WELCOME A – Our Prayer Place B – The Good Shepherd	**1.1 BAPTISM** A – Belonging B – The Sacrament of Baptism	**2.1 IMAGES OF GOD** A – God is Like … B – In the Image of God C – Time With God
K.2 LENT AND HOLY WEEK A – The Lost Sheep B – The Washing of the Feet C – The Last Supper	**1.2 LENT AND HOLY WEEK** A – A Journey From Ashes B – A Journey to Remember	**2.2 LENT AND HOLY WEEK** A – Ash Wednesday and Lent B – Holy Week
K.3 THE EASTER SEASON A – He is Risen! B – Jesus is Alive	**1.3 THE EASTER SEASON** A – Alleluia, Jesus is Alive B – The Ascension C – The Holy Spirit Comes	**2.3 THE EASTER SEASON** A – The Women at the Tomb B – Jesus, Light of the World C – Pentecost People
K.4 BELONGING TO GOD'S PEOPLE A – We Visit the Church B – We Gather for Mass	**1.4 NOURISHED BY GOD** A – Together at Mass B – To Love and Serve	**2.4 SIGNS OF GOD'S LOVE** A – The Church's Year B – Water of Life C – Symbols of the Church
K.5 GOD'S GREAT FAMILY A – Abraham and Sarah B – Jesus' Family	**1.5 STORIES OF GOD'S PEOPLE** A – The Bible B – Called by God	**2.5 REFLECTING GOD'S GOODNESS** A – The Commandment of Love, B – Saints
K.6 GOD IS WITH US A – The Birth of Moses B – David C – Jonah	**1.6 LOVE ONE ANOTHER** A – Living as Friends B – Forgiveness C – Giving Thanks	**2.6 RECONCILIATION** A – The Prodigal Son B – The Sacrament of Penance
K.7 GOD'S CREATION A – Praising God B – God's Promise	**1.7 CREATOR GOD** A – In the Beginning B – Sabbath Time	**2.7 CARING FOR ALL CREATION** A – Who is my Neighbour? B – With All Creation
K.8 ADVENT AND CHRISTMAS A – Waiting and Getting Ready B – The Christmas Story	**1.8 ADVENT AND CHRISTMAS** A – Mary Said 'Yes' B – Jesus is Born	**2.8 ADVENT AND CHRISTMAS** A – Waiting and Hoping B – A New Light

Questions:

1. What is your analysis of the content overview given above? Is it comprehensive?
2. Are there any areas that are not included and should be?
3. Are any areas over represented?

One key difference between RE and other curricula in the school are the forces that shape and direct it. One example of this is that RE curriculum designs draw heavily on Church documents as source material. The RE curriculum in Catholic schools is not something that individual schools make up or elaborate on haphazardly, it is a document of the Church that draws on a range of writings such as the Catechism of the Catholic Church, various Roman or Vatican documents on education and related disciplines and statements from bishops and educational agencies. When you examine diocesan curriculum documents they often include explicit links to Church documents in sections which highlight how the curriculum meets the doctrinal demands expected of it.

Below is part of the doctrinal schema proved by the Archdiocese of Hobart for its RE curriculum document *Good News for Living* (Level 3, Grades 3 and 4).

- We are all created in God's image.
- The Scriptures contain many stories and images that give us some insights into the mystery of God.
- God trusts and forgives us.
- God calls us to reach out in love to each other.
- We are gifted and graced, able to share in the transforming love of God.
- The father of Jesus is our father too.
- The Holy Spirit enables us to live in communication with God and other people.

Activity 6.2: *Find the points listed above on the Hobart Catholic Education Office website. Each point is cross-referenced with the Catechism of the Catholic Church. Match up each point with a Catechism reference and describe the link between the two.*

Another feature of diocesan curriculum documents on religious education is their use of pedagogical models which are included to guide the teaching and learning process. These models are intended to provide a guide for the teacher in the classroom. There are, again, a variety of these models in use. Each is based on a particular approach to the learning process. One of the earliest and most important pedagogical models was the four-fold catechetical process used in the Guidelines for Religious Education of students in the Archdiocese of Melbourne. The four-fold Melbourne process has influenced a generation of RE curriculum planners.

Activity 6.3: *The four fold process.*
Develop a lesson on a topic of your choosing at a particular year level that uses the following four stages:

1. *Experience shared – we share our experience.*
2. *Reflection deepened – we reflect together.*
3. *Faith expressed – we come to know our Catholic faith.*
4. *Insights reinforced – we gain further insights and respond.*

Diocesan curriculum documents also provide a range of unit outlines. These provide much more than ideas for teaching and learning. They often contain background notes for teachers, references to Scripture, learning outcomes, lists of useful resources and extensive links to other related resources. Below is an abbreviated unit outline from the *To Know Worship and Love* Year 3 curriculum from the Archdiocese of Sydney.

Unit 3.4 Pentecost: The Holy Spirit Gives Us Strength

This unit explores the presence of the Holy Spirit in our lives. It focuses on the Holy Spirit as the source of strength, enabling us to continue the mission of Jesus. The unit looks at the Holy Spirit as the fulfillment of Jesus' promise not to leave us alone after he had ascended into Heaven. The unit concludes by identifying the mystery of the Holy Trinity as central to our faith.

Each unit then lists:

- Syllabus Outcomes
- Classroom Outcomes
- Scripture Doctrine
- Values and Attitudes
- Knowledge & Understandings
- Skills
- Ideas for Liturgy and Celebration
- Reference to the Catechism of the Catholic Church
- Resources

Below is some of the background and ideas for teaching and learning from Unit Two from this same document.

The Coming of the Spirit Gave the Disciples Strength to Continue Jesus' Mission of Love and Service

Students will learn:

- about the transformation in the disciples after receiving the Holy Spirit at Pentecost
- to identify the key qualities of the early Christian community.

Background Information

The Pentecost Experience

Prior to the day of Pentecost the disciples were paralysed with fear. They knew on one level what Jesus had asked them to do, yet, faced with the absence of Jesus and the fear of their own persecution, they seemed unable to answer Jesus' call. The task seemed too challenging without Jesus. The coming of the Holy Spirit at Pentecost gave them the strength they needed to carry on the mission of Jesus.

The Feast of Pentecost

The Easter mystery is the Passion, death, and Resurrection of Jesus and the outpouring of the Holy Spirit. As such, the Feast of Pentecost (Pentecost Sunday) concludes the Easter Season. Pentecost is the promise of Jesus fulfilled. Through the Pentecost experience we see that the coming of the Holy Spirit inspires and strengthens the disciples to embody the mission of Jesus. The strength of the Holy Spirit creates the enthusiasm and wisdom to live as Jesus did.

Throughout the history of the Church the duration of the Easter season and the celebration of the Feast of Pentecost have altered. In 1969 the Roman calendar was reformed, returning to the original form of the period between Easter and Pentecost as a period of sustained rejoicing. Prior to this the Sundays during the Easter season were known as the Sundays **after** Easter. Now they are known as the Sundays **of** Easter.

Suggested Teaching/Learning Strategies

- Share the Pentecost event from the *To Know Worship and Love*, Year 3, p. 64 (Acts 2: 1–8). What were the disciples now able to do with the gift of the Holy Spirit? List the actions of the disciples which show that the Holy Spirit had given them strength.

- Invite students to imagine that they are one of the characters in the crowd watching the disciples on the day of Pentecost. Write about what they have witnessed (e.g. the change in the disciples, what they may have seen or heard coming from the room upstairs).
    - The first thing I noticed …
    - What I heard …
    - What I saw …
    - How I felt about what was happening …
    - From reading about the day of Pentecost what do I learn about God?

- Explore the term 'community'. How do people in a community work together and share common interests and belongings? Identify what unites a community. Write definitions for the term 'community'.

- Explain to the students how the apostles continued the work/mission of Jesus and how those who believed formed communities.

- Read Acts 4: 32–35. Discuss what united the early Christian community.

- After reading Acts 4: 32–35 students write a card to the apostles as if they were one of the people in the early Christian community, thanking the apostles for their help and support.

- Identify and list the activities of the early Christian community. Refer to Worksheet 1 (provided).
    - They worked together.
    - They shared their possessions.
    - They believed in Jesus and tried to follow his actions.

- Students write a response to the question: What does Acts 4: 32–35 teach us about being a community?

SHARED CHRISTIAN PRAXIS

Many diocese have adapted an approach to religious education originally devised by Thomas Groome from Boston College in the United States, known as Shared Christian Praxis. By *praxis* Groome (1991) means action-reflection, or reflective action, highlighting the dynamic and interrelated activities of thinking and acting. The theory behind this approach is somewhat complex, and anecdotal evidence suggests that many teachers do not utilize Shared Christian Praxis in the manner intended because they do not really have an understanding of the theoretical underpinnings.

While space does not permit in this book to present a detailed explanation of the theory behind this approach, it is possible to present a brief outline of the stages, or movements, which comprise this methodology. Following an initial focusing activity designed to draw the attention of the students to the topic of interest, Groome outlines five movements in this process:

- Naming the present action (a reflection upon present events and a distinction made between what is really happening and what should be happening);
- The participants' stories and visions in relation to the present action (the beginning of critical reflection on the factors that have led to the present situation. It is concerned with the 'why' questions, for example, 'why do we do as we do?');
- Presentation of the story and vision of the Christian community (Aspects of the Christian story are remembered and told. Participants are provided with an opportunity to see their own experience in the light of the Christian vision);
- Dialogue between the Christian story and the participant' stories (In light of remembering the Christian story, the participants' experiences are examined in light of what 'should be' as well as what actually 'is');
- A decision for future action (out of an understanding of the way it was and the way it should have been can emerge a decision to close the gap between the lived experience and the Christian vision. This is the point at which praxis is considered to have developed).

In essence then, this approach centers on a sharing of the stories and experiences of the participants, including the teacher or facilitator, which are directed towards a response in faith to the Christian story. It is an approach which has been considered as academically challenging and rigorous in that an emphasis is placed on critical self reflection by initiating the participants to think in a praxis model rather than to learn theories. However, there have been critics of this approach who maintain that it does not have a place in the compulsory religion classroom where students have not come together freely to share faith (e.g. Ryan, 1998). Nonetheless, Shared Christian Praxis continues to hold a predominant place in religious education in many dioceses in Australia and elsewhere.

Activity 6.4

Log onto the following website for the Catholic Education Office for the Archdiocese of Canberra-Goulburn:
http://www.ceo.cg.catholic.edu.au/re/tno/document/core_section4.pdf

What does this document say about Shared Christian Praxis?

FURTHER QUESTIONS AND ACTIVITIES

1. Each diocese and Catholic Education Office usually has its own website. Locate one such website and explore the unit outlines provided by this diocese.

2. Log onto the Diocese of Ballarat website: http://www.web.ceo.balrt.catholic.edu.au/. What is the learning and teaching approach used for early years' classrooms?

3. Using the religious education curriculum documents that form the basis of RE in your own diocese, list the various components that comprise the foundational elements for the suggested units of work. How important is it that teachers be familiar with these elements?

REFERENCES

Catholic Education Office, Hobart. (2005). *Good news for living*. Hobart: Catholic Education Office, Archdiocese of Hobart.

Elliott, P. (Ed.). (2002). *To know, worship and love* series. Melbourne: James Goold House.

Groome, T. (1991). *Sharing faith; A comprehensive approach to religious education and pastoral ministry*. San Francisco: HarperCollins.

Ryan, M. (2006). *Religious education in Catholic schools: An introduction for Australian students*. Melbourne: David Lovell.

CHAPTER 7

WHAT DO I DO IF THIS HAPPENS? DEALING WITH SOME DIFFICULT ISSUES IN CLASSROOM RELIGIOUS EDUCATION

Questions:

1. Do you have any anxieties about teaching religious education?
2. Are these different from general concerns about your teaching career?
3. If so, what are the specific issues around RE?

It is important that new teachers are not discouraged from teaching religious education (RE) because they are anxious about how they will cope in the classroom. Many teachers, especially inexperienced ones, often have an exaggerated fear about the problems that may arise in RE. In a school with a well-thought-out and implemented RE curriculum and where the teachers are well versed in their professional responsibilities the focus of classroom RE tends to be on meeting educational goals. By having this focus problems that arise can be dealt with within the context of the ethos of Catholic schools. By understanding some of the issues that may arise and how to respond well, the new RE teacher can work with confidence in the classroom and in the wider school. If teachers are prepared to discuss their concerns when they arise with the relevant people in the school, be they the Religious Education Coordinator (REC) or members of the school's leadership team, then difficulties can be minimised.

Questions:

1. In your experience of Catholic schools what are some of the difficulties that arise in RE classes?
2. How would you rank these in terms of seriousness?
3. Which are the most frequent?

TALKING THINGS OVER

Casey: *I am really looking forward to teaching, but RE worries me a bit. I'm just not confident; I mean, I don't know anything about it.*
Meagan: *Yeah, me too. I mean, what are sacraments and all the other stuff?*
Sam: *What about some of the questions the kids can ask? I just wouldn't know what to say.*
Luke: *And there are also lifestyle issues; how much of it are you supposed to take personally?*
Sarah: *I've heard that schools check up on you to see how you are living. And the parish priest can be a real tyrant.*
Kate: *Don't get too paranoid. Schools respect your private life as long as you keep it private. What they are interested in is how you teach and interact with students.*
Meagan: *Schools are really learning focused. I'm sure once you get into schools there will be lots of assistance available.*
Casey: *I think you're right. When I was doing my observations the school was great and gave the new teachers terrific support, especially in RE.*
Luke: *Gee, I don't think so. At the school I was at RE didn't seem to work at all. There was not a lot of quality teaching and learning going on. The RE teaching was just not challenging.*
Marina: *What if you make a mistake and get parents calling in and giving you a hard time?*
Meagan: *Yeah, and in RE can't the parish priest get involved? And what if he is a tyrant?*

Imagine that you are listening to the following conversation. Who do you most identify with?

Issue Number 1:

Content knowledge and RE – *I just don't know anything about it.*

In the dialogue above Casey expressed that her greatest anxiety about teaching RE was a lack of content knowledge. Meagan agreed with her. This is a good example of an issue that troubles many new RE teachers. In recent years classroom RE teaching has placed more emphasis on the educational goals of RE. If you want to help students understand more about the Catholic tradition, or any other for that matter, then you need to have a strong grasp of the content of RE. There is no way of avoiding this. If, for example, you are involved in teaching about a sacramental program, you need to have a good grasp of the theology behind the Eucharist in order to convey this to students.

If the RE teacher wants to teach well within an educational approach they must prepare themselves with background information about the topics they are teaching. This is especially true when teachers take upon themselves the responsibility of speaking for the Tradition. This is a very necessary role for the RE teacher. For example, when a teacher says *the Catholic Church teaches* … he or she is making an objective statement. These are to be encouraged because they give students a firm position on which their own understanding can grow. Nonetheless, it is the responsibility of the RE teacher to be accurate when making objective statements. If unsure about statements on behalf of the Tradition check with others, such as the REC or other suitably qualified people. Do your homework thoroughly before you approach a new or unfamiliar topic. RE teachers need to approach complex issues with caution. They can get into some difficulty by launching into areas which require careful preparation and background reading.

To be prepared does not mean that to teach RE well you need to have a post-graduate qualification in theology, scripture or religious education. This is not to say these would not help, and many teachers take on extra studies to improve their knowledge base. Most RECs have such post-graduate qualifications or are in the process of getting them. In many dioceses this is required to take up a leadership position in RE. Classroom teachers, especially early in their career, can gain a good insight into topics by directed reading. Most RE curricula have notes for teachers which distil much of the main points in the area. Be prepared also to speak to the leadership team at the school for what assistance is available at the school level.

Issue Number 2:

What would you do if a student asked a hard but legitimate question in the RE class?

You could also put the issue that Sam raises under the heading of content knowledge. Students can ask some really tough questions. 'Is this wrong?', 'Why does God let this happen?', and 'Did Adam and Eve really exist?' are some examples. If students ask you questions then take this as a compliment. Research shows that students do this when they have some faith in your ability as a teacher and feel comfortable in your presence. It also means that it is likely that you have created a strong learning environment in your classroom. Some of the questions that come up in RE are complex. Do not feel that you have to come up with all the answers to the great questions of life. It is acceptable to take some questions 'on notice' and get back to students. As your confidence grows and your understanding of content areas improves you will find that you can give students credible answers to many questions.

Other questions may arise spontaneously on issues that are topical at the time. These may come up in the electronic media and hence have a very wide circulation. One example of such material is the issue of clerical sexual abuse. How should an inexperienced RE teacher deal with issues like this? If discussion arises in the course of a lesson some further comment is appropriate. Certainly an expression of sorrow and an acknowledgment of the deep hurt that has been caused can be made. Depending on the age of the students some deeper analysis can also be given. There is, however, no easy answer to many current and topical issues. It is unlikely that discussing them at great length will assist in resolution or significant progress. There is also the danger that the purposeful teaching of the RE curriculum will be disrupted if too much attention is given to issues as they arise. The RE teacher should be responsive to student enquiries about issues of the day; however, this should not become the main focus of the RE classroom. It is not advisable to allow the RE classroom to become dominated by discussion of issues that have arisen in the most recent blockbuster movie or segment on current affairs shows. Ideally many of these topics could be discussed within the existing RE curriculum where they can be placed in an appropriate educational context.

Issue Number 3:

Help at the school – *I'm sure once you get into schools there will be lots of assistance available.*

In the dialogue above Casey and Luke have different experiences of the amount of support given to new RE teachers in schools. Fortunately, Casey's experience is the norm. Most schools have a strong commitment to RE and do a good deal to help teachers, especially those who are new to the profession. Most schools have experienced teachers in leadership positions in RE. This person is usually the REC or someone in a similar position. Part of their job is to help RE teachers, and this includes new staff when the need arises. New RE teachers can make situations more difficult for themselves if they do not communicate regularly with the REC. Some issues that arise in the contemporary RE class can be difficult for an inexperienced teacher to deal with alone. These are not problems, however, that occur in isolation, and are dealt with on a school basis. They have been faced before and can be dealt with effectively provided concerned parties are informed about what is going on.

Issue Number 4:

Expectations of parents – *What if you make a mistake and get parents calling in and giving you a hard time?*

The basic advice here is to make sure that you are familiar with the school's RE program, and if difficulties arise promptly inform the REC. Difficulties here could include being contacted by a parent directly about something that has occurred in your RE class. For example, a parent may raise concerns over the sacramental program and suggest that the children are being presented something which is contrary to Catholic teaching. Or another parent may want the school to keep up with the times and teach something which is not in accord with the Catholic tradition. It is important for the new RE teacher to be aware that the religious education program in the school is not something that is fashioned by the school alone. In Catholic primary schools the RE program is controlled and authorised, ultimately, by the bishop. In the Catholic tradition it is the bishop, not the teacher or the parent, who is the final authority on whether something conforms to Catholic teaching or not. Teachers working in Catholic schools can be confident that what is in the school's religious education curriculum conforms to Catholic teaching because it has been approved by the bishop through agencies such as Catholic Education Offices which work under his mandate. Because of this parents cannot ask the school to present material in religious education that is not in accord with what the Church teaches.

Bear in mind that if parents express an interest in what goes on in the RE class this is a positive thing. If misunderstandings occur they can usually be corrected with better communication. Parents with obvious interest in the religious education of their child should be encouraged and welcomed. Consulting with the parent usually results in a satisfactory outcome.

Issue Number 5:

Parish interface – *What if the parish priest is a real tyrant?*

Catholic primary schools are almost always associated with a local parish. Because of this the parish priest is a vital figure in both the parish and the school. Parish priests are very interested in providing a quality education for all the children in the school. It has been the clear experience of most primary schools that the parish priest is a great support to religious education in the school. Schools and parishes work very closely on a range of issues, but perhaps nowhere is this more evident than in preparing children for the sacraments. Students are usually prepared for these in schools, and then receive the sacraments, such as the Eucharist, in the parish.

Recognise the key role of the parish priest. In Catholic schools he is not a tangential figure. Realise as well that, as in any human relationship, there is the possibility for friction. There are many reasons for this, but among parish priests and inexperienced RE teachers there are the usual quotas of difficult personalities or people who do not respond at their best all of the time. If difficulties arise it is best to identify these early, and raise concerns with key people in the school, such as the principal. The golden rule of 'speak to someone at the school when problems arise' can certainly be used here.

Issue Number 6:

Professional responsibilities and the private lives of RE teachers – *... lifestyle issues, how much of it are you supposed to take personally?*

Luke has raised the issue of the relationship between the professional and personal lives of RE teachers. What are the boundaries of the personal lives of RE teachers? This question is not restricted to RE, but affects all teachers who work in Catholic schools.

Questions:

1. What do you see as the boundaries around the personal life of the teacher?
2. What are some of the issues that are brought up by this case?

Source document 1:

Lay Catholics in Schools: Witnesses to Faith.

The teacher under discussion here is not simply a professional person who systematically transmits a body of knowledge in the context of a school; 'teacher' is to be understood as 'educator' – one who helps to form human persons. The task of a teacher goes well beyond transmission of knowledge, although that is not excluded. Therefore, if adequate professional preparation is required in order to transmit knowledge, then adequate professional preparation is even more necessary in order to fulfill the role of a genuine teacher. It is an indispensable human formation, and without it, it would be foolish to undertake any educational work.

One specific characteristic of the educational profession assumes its most profound significance in the Catholic educator: the communication of truth. For the Catholic educator, whatever is true is a participation in Him who is the Truth; the communication of truth, therefore, as a professional activity, is thus fundamentally transformed into a unique participation in the prophetic mission of Christ, carried on through one's teaching.

LCS: WF 16

Questions:

1. What implications does this extract have for teachers in Catholic schools?
2. What is your response to this quote?

Ford (1986) discusses the professional responsibilities and the private lives of teachers in Catholic schools. He states 'Undoubtedly the known behaviour of a teacher both in and out of school could affect the moral outlook of his/her pupils for the better or the worse'. This is why the new RE teacher should understand the professional and personal dimensions of teaching. The area of the private life of the teacher is one for the individuals involved. The school has no right to enquire about these matters provided they remain out of the public domain. More to the point, students have no right to ask about these matters. Teachers who allow themselves to be quizzed by students about how they choose to live their lives are not respecting the boundaries of proper professional teacher conduct. Recognise that if you choose to work in a Catholic school then you are agreeing to work within the parameters of a certain tradition and ethos. You are of course under no obligation to work in the Catholic school system.

As part of their professional lives teachers must respect the integrity of the school and its relationship with the Church. Catholic schools are integral parts of the mission and function of the Church. People who work in schools are expected not to contradict what the Church teaches, since this forms a vital part of the ethos of the school. This is especially important for RE teachers in the classroom. Mutual respect is called for. It also speaks to the professionalism of the teacher. If the RE teacher does not agree with a particular aspect of Church teaching this remains his or her own opinion, but this should not become a forum for disagreement, which can disrupt the culture and atmosphere of the school. In other words, the classroom is not the place for the RE teacher to air his or her disagreements with the Church.

SOURCE DOCUMENT 2:

The Catholic School on the Threshold of the Third Millennium.

In the Catholic school, 'prime responsibility for creating this unique Christian school climate rests with the teachers, as individuals and as a community'. Teaching has an extraordinary moral depth and is one of man's most excellent and creative activities, for the teacher does not write on inanimate material, but on the very spirits of human beings. The personal relations between the teacher and the students, therefore, assume an enormous importance and are not limited simply to giving and taking. Moreover, we must remember that teachers and educators fulfill a specific Christian vocation and share an equally specific participation in the mission of the Church, to the extent that 'it depends chiefly on them whether the Catholic school achieves its purpose'.

CSTTM, 19

Questions:

1. What do you think is the extraordinary moral depth of teaching?
2. How is the contribution of teachers to Catholic schools described?
3. How are students described above?

Activity 7.1: At the start of this chapter you were asked, 'Do you have any anxieties about teaching religious education?' How would you respond now?

REFERENCES

The Sacred Congregation for Catholic Education. (1982). *Lay Catholics in schools: Witnesses to faith* (16). Homebush, NSW: St Paul Publications.

Congregation for Catholic Education. (1997). *The Catholic school on the threshold of the Third Millennium* (19). Homebush, NSW: St Paul Publications.

Ford, N. (1986). *Professional responsibility and the private lives of teachers in Catholic schools*. Homebush: St Paul Publications.

Rymarz, R. (1999). Knowledge and the RE teacher. *Journal of Religious Education 47*(4), 48-54.

CHAPTER 8

PERSONAL AND LITURGICAL PRAYER WITH EARLY YEARS' STUDENTS

Prayer is a catechetical activity. It assumes faith commitment, and so is usually something that is undertaken either individually by a person who has faith, or it is undertaken by groups of people who are already disciples or followers of Jesus, and who share a common faith. Many would therefore argue that the *insistence* of prayer within the religious education classroom is not appropriate because it cannot be assumed that the students are committed believers (for example, Ryan, 2006).

However, providing *opportunities* for both liturgical and personal prayer is an appropriate undertaking, particularly within the Catholic school as a whole, but also such opportunities can be provided within the religious education classroom, provided that they are *invitational*. This chapter focuses specifically on personal and liturgical prayer in early years' classrooms. It outlines some pertinent considerations for the religious educator in planning opportunities for such experiences, and it suggests one possible structure around which to plan appropriate experiences of prayer and ritual.

WHAT IS PRAYER?

In essence, prayer is a communication between God and humankind which encompasses all dimensions of life – the joys and sorrows, the times of affirmation, and the times when forgiveness and healing are sought (Healy, Hyde & Rymarz, 2004). In prayer, especially prayer which is centered on the Word of God, people are transformed in order to transform the world. Prayer is both individual and communal. It may be focused on individual needs but it is grounded in the community and connected with the world. Prayer may involve silence, song, gesture, movement, drama, the spoken word and the recitation of communal prayers. It may involve silent reflection and contemplation as well as noise. Good experiences of prayer are sensory in that they involve as many of the sense as are possible – sight, sound, smell, touch, and even taste.

In the early years' classroom, it is possible to include many of these components of prayer. However, in order to ensure that opportunities for prayer do not become "cluttered" or simply times when "anything and everything goes", it is suggested that classroom prayer has structure. This structure may follow closely the pattern of the Eucharist, and would thus contain the elements of Gathering, Word, Symbol/Response and Commissioning. The following section outlines one possible structure around which to plan appropriate experience of classroom prayer in early years' settings.

A STRUCTURE FOR CLASSROOM PRAYER IN EARLY YEARS' SETTINGS

The structure suggested here has been adapted from several sources (for example, Bretherton, 1995, Wintour, 1998) and is appropriate for use as a guide when planning opportunities for prayer with young children in early years' classrooms. The structure contains four elements:

- Gathering
- Listening
- Responding
- Go and Tell (commissioning)

Each of these elements represents an adaptation of the pattern of the Eucharist, and so this type of prayer is sometimes referred to as Liturgical Prayer. Because children in early years' classrooms have not usually celebrated their First Eucharist (at least, not in their first year of formal schooling), many teachers prefer to plan Liturgical Prayer rather than a class Mass. Because they have not celebrated First Eucharist, they cannot come to the Table. It is a little like preparing a great feast or party, leading the children to the table, but turning them away hungry!

When planning Liturgical Prayer, the starting point is **not** with the element of Gathering, but rather with the element of Listening.

Listening

When planning Liturgical Prayer, we begin by identifying and locating the Scripture passage that will be used. The Scripture story selected, and the theme of that particular story, will color how each of the other elements of the prayer are planned. For example, if the Scripture passage chosen is "The Call of the First Disciples" (Mark 1: 14-20), the theme could be something along the lines of "Following Jesus" or perhaps "Following in Jesus' Footsteps". As we shall see in a moment, this theme will color the planning of each of the other elements of the Liturgical Prayer structure.

Usually, the Scripture passage would come from the Gospel stories. This is because the Person of Jesus is central for Christians. Therefore, all of the events which comprise and culminate in the life, death and resurrection of Jesus as contained in the four Gospel accounts provide appropriate Scripture passages for Christians as the basis of prayerful experiences. However, there are passages from Hebrew Scripture which may also be appropriate, particularly if, for example, the focus of your Liturgical Prayer is to center on "Creation".

Having chosen the desired passage of Scripture, it is important to consider how the children will listen, that is, how the Word will be proclaimed. Will it simply be read, and by whom? Could it be dramatized using a resource such as "The Dramatized Bible"? Could the story be proclaimed using puppets? Will there be more than one voice involved in the proclamation? Will there be a procession of the Word? Will students be invited to use an appropriate Gospel Acclamation (Alleluia)? Will this procession be accompanied by candles? There are many possibilities here that require careful and deliberate discernment by the educator.

Having selected and examined the Scripture passage, it is now possible to plan each of the other elements of the Liturgical Prayer celebration. These will be influenced by the choice Scripture reading, as we shall now see.

Gathering

At Sunday Mass, the gathering actually begins from the moment people leave their homes and begin to physically gather in the Church. It includes things like parking the car in the Church grounds, greeting others as people enter the Church, as well as the more formal liturgical elements such as the Entrance Song, the Sign of the Cross, and the Opening Prayer. So, when planning Liturgical Prayer for the classroom context, it is important to give some consideration as to how the class will gather. For example, if the theme is "Following in Jesus' Footsteps", it might be that from the classroom, you are planning to gather in a quiet space somewhere else in the school. Particular students could be charged with the responsibility of standing up and calling (at a time agreed upon by the students and yourself) "Follow Me!" These students would then motion to four or five students to literally follow them to the prepared prayer space. This might be repeated a few moments apart by different students, so that groups of students actually follow those who made the call to the prayer space. The students who call "Follow me!" could also lead the students to the prepared prayer space by different paths.

Once gathered in the prayer space, a gathering prayer, song, or perhaps both could be said/sung by all who have gathered as a sign of Gathering. In continuing with the theme "Following in Jesus' Footsteps", one appropriate song might be Christopher Walker's "Fishing for People", from the collection "Stories and Songs about Jesus". But notice how the Scripture passage and its theme have influenced how the Gathering has been organized.

Responding

Having gathered and Listened to God's Word, an opportunity needs to be planned for the students to respond in some way. The response could take the form of silence if appropriate. It could involve song. It could involve lighting a candle, or some other action which the students physically do. For example, considering the theme "Following in Jesus' Footsteps", students could write/draw on a footprint stencil, one way in which they might respond to the call of Jesus to follow in their own lives.

At Sunday Mass, one of the ways in which the congregation responds to the Gospel is through the Prayers of the Faithful (Prayers of Intercession) in which, having listened to God's Word, the congregation places their needs before the Lord. If you listen carefully to these Prayers of the Faithful, you will notice that they are not simply made up. They come from the theme of the Gospel story which has been proclaimed. In the classroom Liturgical Prayer, it is also possible to respond to the Word through Prayers of Intercession which emanate from the theme of the Gospel. For example, if the theme is "Following in Jesus' Footsteps", the following could be examples of Prayers of Intercession which reflect this theme:

> Prayer: Lord Jesus, you call us to follow you. Help us to live more like you.
> Response: *Jesus, help us to follow you.*
>
> Prayer: Lord Jesus, you call us to follow you. Help us to be friendly to others in the playground.
> Response: *Jesus, help us to follow you.*
>
> Prayer: Lord Jesus, you call us to follow you. Help us to be loving brothers and sisters and children
> Response: *Jesus, help us to follow you.*

Go and Tell

Sunday Mass concludes not with a statement like "see you all next week," but rather with a commissioning to "Go in peace to love and serve the Lord". This is in fact a command to go out and to live what has been proclaimed in the Gospel. The Gospel story ought to have touched our hearts and challenged us to live differently in our everyday lives.

The "Go and Tell" element of this structure attempts to issue this same challenge to students. Having listened and responded to God's Word as proclaimed in Scripture, students are challenged to live this Word in their daily lives, albeit simply and basically. Taking the theme "Following in Jesus' Footsteps", this element could be captured in a short commissioning prayer in which children are challenged to live more like Jesus by deciding upon one thing they might change in their lives to reflect this challenge. It doesn't need to be something "earth-shattering". It could be as simple as deciding to tolerate a sibling who can be annoying, or by trying not to tease another child when tempted to do so.

Often, song and music are used to capture this element. There are a number of appropriate songs which can be used here, including Christopher Walker's "Take the Word of God" and Monica Brown's "Go now in peace". These two examples have been composed specifically with children in mind. There are, however, many other possibilities.

Following is a proforma which may be helpful in planning Liturgical Prayer.

Proforma for Liturgical Prayer

Theme of the Prayer	
Venue	

Element:	What you will do:
Gathering Consider: space (where?), music, silence…	
Listening Consider: Scripture passage, the proclamation (read, dramatized, puppets, use of voice, Gospel Acclamation (Alleluia)…	
Responding Consider: action, movement, Prayers of Intercession, music…	
Go and Tell Consider: taking the Word to the world, commissioning, music, action outside the classroom…	

OTHER CONSIDERATIONS

In exploring each of the above elements there are also other considerations. For example the environment – where will this Liturgical Prayer experience be held? Is the environment conducive to prayer? How will an ambiance be created? Will the layout of the space allow room for procession and gesture? Can I subdue the lighting? It may be that the classroom space, for one reason or another, is not the best place to hold a Liturgical Prayer celebration. It may also be that the Parish Church is not conducive for a small gathering because it is too big a space for a small class of students, and is not intimate enough. Choose the environment carefully.

Also, is it possible to prepare a prayer focus? In taking the theme "Following in Jesus' Footsteps", a prayer focus/symbol could include some colored material, a candle and perhaps a pair of sandals. The prayer focus/symbol should not be cluttered with items, but should provide a focal point, enabling children to center their attention.

If music is to be used, what type? Will it include quite reflective "background" music? Will it include songs? Will these be recorded or can the students use instruments or just their voices? There are at present a plethora of excellent children's liturgical music compilations, composed by experienced musicians and liturgists, which are easily accessible in both school and parish communities, and which can be purchased through world-wide distributors, such as Pauline Books and Media.

Allow sufficient time for students to be given the opportunity to enter the experience of prayer. Do not rush things. Do not be afraid of silence or of slowing the tempo down. Prayer takes as long as it takes. If students are to read, teach them to slow their reading, and allow them time to practice to master this skill.

PERSONAL PRAYER

The General Directory for Catechesis maintains that one of the major aims of catechetical activity is "to challenge students to permeate the whole of their life with a spirit of prayer, and so discover the mysterious action of God, who gives us strength in our weakness" (GDC, #85). Opportunities should be provided to students for openness to God through personal prayer. Relationship with God in prayer ideally enables the young child to develop in their inner capacity for creativity and wonder and to be responsive to their own needs and the needs of others.

The development of an individual life of prayer may be assisted by learning the prayers of the Church and the prayers of the Liturgy. Many schools have developed a Prayer Policy to ensure that formal prayers are introduced when student are at an appropriate stage of readiness.

However, there are many other types and styles of prayer, aside from the prayers of the Church, which are appropriate for students in early years' classrooms. While it is beyond the scope of this chapter to outline the numerous possibilities for personal prayer, there are many publications which have been produced in recent years which achieve this purpose. For example, Barbara Bretherton (1995, 1997, 1999) has three published books which outline a number of valuable prayer strategies and styles which are applicable to children of all ages, and many of which have immediate relevance and application for children in early years' classrooms. Nolan's (1999) publication also contains a wealth of excellent ideas for prayer.

When planning personal prayer, many of the considerations for Liturgical Prayer similarly apply. An environment conducive for prayer needs to be established. This will involve a consideration of lighting, the position of classroom furniture, the use of music or perhaps silence to create an ambience, perhaps even the use of an oil burner or fragrant incense.

As with Liturgical prayer, ensure sufficient time for children has been given for the opportunity to enter the experience of prayer. Do not be afraid of periods of silence, or of providing opportunities for children to experience silence as an element of the prayer experience. Silence is an integral element in prayer, and one that is often absent in lives of children today because of the frantic pace of life in western culture. Yet, some silence is essential in experiences of prayer. It is a valuable skill to be mastered, and, in today's world, a skill that needs to be taught and practiced.

CONCLUSION

The invitation and opportunity to pray is a relevant inclusion in early years' religious education classrooms. This chapter has provided one possible structure for classroom experiences of prayer in which the Word of God – Scripture – has a prominent place.

FURTHER QUESTIONS AND ACTIVITIES

1. Do you think that prayer should be included as a part of the classroom religious education program for early years' students? Discuss this with a partner.

2. Imagine that you are planning Liturgical Prayer centered on the Scripture passage in which Jesus calms the storm (Mark 4: 35-41). Use the proforma in this chapter to plan each of the elements of Gathering, Listening, Responding, and Go and Tell.

3. Are there any other considerations you can think of in planning experiences of either Liturgical or personal prayer?

4. Suppose you have children from other Faith Traditions in your classroom. What are the implications of this for planning experiences of prayer?

REFERENCES

Bretherton, B. (1995). *Praying with children: A resource book for primary teachers.* Wentworth Falls, NSW: Social Science Press.

Bretherton, B. (1997). *You, me and God: Prayer themes and guided meditations for children.* Wentworth Falls, NSW: Social Science Press.

Bretherton, B. (1999). *Prayers at your fingertips.* Katoomba, NSW: Social Science Press.

Healy, H., Hyde, B., & Rymarz, R. (2004). *Making our way through primary RE: A handbook for religious educators.* Tuggerah, NSW: Social Science Press.

Nolan, B. (1999). *Prayer strategies: A teacher's manual.* Melbourne: HarperCollins Religious.

Ryan, M. (2006). *Religious education in Catholic schools: An introduction for Australian students.* Melbourne, VIC: David Lovell.

Sacred Congregation for the Clergy. (1997). *General directory for catechesis.* Homebush, NSW: St. Pauls's.

Wintour, R. (1998). *Sacred celebrations: Liturgies for children.* Brisbane: Mountjoy Enterprises.

CHAPTER 9

TEACHING ABOUT SACRAMENTS

Activity 9.1: *How would you describe sacraments? Think this over for a while, and if you have the opportunity discuss it with someone else. Write down your main points.*

One of the distinguishing features of Catholic schools is the emphasis on sacraments. When teachers who are new to the system are asked what sets the Catholic school apart from other schools they have worked in, one of the strongest responses is that in Catholic schools they have the Mass 'all the time'. As well as school masses, liturgical celebrations marking the beginning of the year and other landmarks, sacraments occupy a central place in the RE curriculum of schools.

There are a number of ways to think about sacraments. Sacraments can be described as specific signs of God's presence in the world. They mark the ongoing relationship between God and humanity. People sometimes describe sacraments in terms of duty and obligation, but a stronger way of conceptualising what sacraments are and what they do is to see them as a gift. They are a gift from God and a call to serve God and others. Celebrating the sacraments is also one of the most common and visible expressions of Catholic life. By receiving the sacraments, Catholics build up this relationship with God. This is most obviously seen in the celebration of the Eucharist which is at the heart of Catholic worship. Some sacraments can be received only once because they have a permanent effect, but the Eucharist can be received daily, so it signifies an ongoing relationship. Sacraments often mark the major events in a Catholic's life. From birth to death, and at significant moments in between, sacraments are signs of the presence of God, moments when God changes us and helps us to grow.

Quick Quiz

1. List the seven sacraments of the Church.
2. What are the three categories of sacraments? Give an example of a sacrament in each category.
3. 'Sacraments are described as a gift and a call.' Explain this statement.
4. Sacraments can be described as mysteries. Can we know anything about a mystery?
5. Name three things the Catholic Church teaches about sacraments.

UNDERSTANDING SACRAMENTS

The Latin word *sacramentum* meant a holy oath made in the presence of the gods. The early Christians began to use the word to describe the holy moments that Jesus Christ had chosen to be with them.

Sacraments are visible actions but they also have deeper meaning and supernatural power, which is part of the mystery of God. To say something is mysterious does not mean that we know nothing about it. It means that we do not understand everything about it. What are some of the things the Catholic Church teaches about sacraments?

Catholics believe that God is present and active in this world. God is not a force floating in outer space, billions of miles from us. We come to know God through the person of Jesus Christ because, in Jesus, God became one of us and lived among us and died for us. God became visible in Jesus. This is why Christ is described as the *first sacrament*. Jesus Christ continues to act in the world through the Church. The Church is a sacrament that shows God's love for all people and for all of creation. Catholics believe that the Holy Spirit acts through the Church in a life-giving way, which is called grace. The seven sacraments are visible ways through which the Holy Spirit acts. By participating in and receiving the sacraments, we come closer to Christ, who is present in all of them. The Church celebrates seven sacraments. The sacraments can be grouped into three categories: the sacraments of initiation, healing, and service.

THE SACRAMENTS OF CHRISTIAN INITIATION

SOURCE DOCUMENT 1:

Catechism of the Catholic Church.

At the Last Supper, on the night he was betrayed, our Savior instituted the Eucharistic sacrifice of his Body and Blood. This he did in order to perpetuate the sacrifice of the cross throughout the ages until he should come again, and so to entrust to his beloved Spouse, the Church, a memorial of his death and resurrection: a sacrament of love, a sign of unity, a bond of charity, a Paschal banquet 'in which Christ is consumed, the mind is filled with grace, and a pledge of future glory is given to us'. The Eucharist is 'the source and summit of the Christian life'. The other sacraments, and indeed all ecclesiastical ministries and works of the apostolate, are bound up with the Eucharist and are oriented towards it. For in the blessed Eucharist is contained the whole spiritual good of the Church, namely Christ himself, our Pasch.

CCC 1324-1325

Questions:

1. List two of the ways the Eucharist is described in the extract above.
2. In your own words describe what you think the three main points of the extract are.
3. Why is the Eucharist called the source and summit of Christian life?

Baptism, Confirmation and the Eucharist are the sacraments of Initiation. Baptism and Confirmation lay the foundation of Christian life. Both of these sacraments have a permanent effect and can never be repeated. In these sacraments God is present at the beginning of Christian life and when it reaches maturity. The central sacrament, and the one to which all other sacraments lead, is the Eucharist. The Eucharist is the heart of Catholic life. It recalls and celebrates the death and Resurrection of Jesus Christ and the new covenant between God and his people.

THE SACRAMENTS OF HEALING

SOURCE DOCUMENT 2:

The Gospel of Matthew.

When he came down from the mountain, great crowds followed him and behold, a leper came to him and knelt before him, saying, 'Lord, if you will, you can make me clean'. And he reached out his hand and touched him saying, 'I will; be clean'. And immediately his leprosy was cleansed. And Jesus said to him, 'See that you say nothing to any one; but go show yourself to the priest, and offer the gift that Moses commanded, for a proof for the people'.

Matt 8: 1–4.

Questions:

1. In the extract above how is the leper cleansed?
2. What do you think is the main point of this story?
3. What does this story tell us about Jesus as a healer and his attitude to forgiveness?

Penance and Anointing of the Sick are the sacraments of healing that can be received more than once. These sacraments are a sign that God is present and active in difficult times, such as when we need to be forgiven, or are challenged by illness. Through these sacraments Jesus continues to forgive and heal us.

THE SACRAMENTS OF SERVICE

Marriage and Holy Orders are the sacraments of service. In these sacraments, God is present and active when couples devote themselves to serve each other in married life, and when men respond to the call to serve the people of God as bishops, priests and deacons. Holy Orders has a permanent effect and can never be repeated.

SOURCE DOCUMENT 3:

Gaudium et Spes.

For, God Himself is the author of matrimony, endowed as it is with various benefits and purposes.(1) All of these have a very decisive bearing on the continuation of the human race, on the personal development and eternal destiny of the individual members of a family, and on the dignity, stability, peace and prosperity of the family itself and of human society as a whole. By their very nature, the institution of matrimony itself and conjugal love are ordained for the procreation and education of children, and find in them their ultimate crown. Thus a man and a woman, who by their compact of conjugal love 'are no longer two, but one flesh ' (Matt. 19:ff), render mutual help and service to each other through an intimate union of their persons and of their actions.

GS 48

Questions:

1. Who is the author of matrimony?
2. What are some of the benefits of marriage for society in general?
3. What does marriage give to the partners?

ISSUES IN SACRAMENTAL EDUCATION

Activity 9.2: *'It is the job of the Catholic school to prepare students to celebrate the sacraments.' Discuss this statement.*

Role of the School in Sacramental Education

One of the most important catechetical aspects of Catholic primary schools is their role in preparing children to celebrate sacraments. In most Catholic schools sacramental programs make up an important part of the religious education curriculum from the early years' through until the end of primary school. When you analyse the amount of time that Catholic schools devote to teaching about sacraments in their programs, they are clearly a major educational focus. Many parishes also run programs; often these are directed towards children who are not attending Catholic schools. While the school or parish team has an important role to play here it needs to be said that the main locus of catechetical formation of children is the faith community into which they are born. Church documents are quite clear on this point: the first educators of children are parents, and this is especially so when it comes to faith formation. If faith formation is not occurring in the home then the school cannot fully compensate for this, despite excellent educational programs and ample opportunities for faith expression.

Activity 9.3: Meagan is a keen and well prepared religious education teacher. She is aware that her school has an excellent sacramental program for students preparing to celebrate Holy Communion for the first time. Having taught this for a few years, she is sometimes a little despondent that although the students in her class respond well this does not lead to a change in their behavior. They do not go to Mass regularly. This makes her feel at times that she has failed in her role.

What advice would you give to Meagan?

SOME APPROACHES TO TEACHING SACRAMENTS TO CHILDREN

1. Using the Experiential World of the Child

All students learn within a particular social context and access prior learning in their attempts to integrate new information. When teaching about sacraments in Catholic schools it is important to recognise this in classroom practice. This may be as simple as asking students for their recollections about a family gathering or another specific occasion. It can be more directed, asking them to give their experience of being at a baptism or the wedding of a sibling or family member. In the case of ordination or an anointing service it may be necessary to create stories about these, or to use audiovisual aids to assist your teaching, as students may have little or no experience of being part of them.

Scenario 1: We know nothing!

Casey is taking a Year 6 class and the topic is Confirmation, with most of the students preparing to receive the sacrament later in the year. She begins her first class on the topic with a question, 'Who can tell me something about sacraments?' She is met with a stony silence – her next move is …

By the time students have reached the end of Catholic primary school they have done seven years of RE. If we assume that schools offer a strong curriculum focus which emphasise the educational goals of the subject then it can be expected that most students have already done a good deal about sacraments. Despite what they may say students have a good deal of prior leaning on the topic, and the task of the skilful teacher is to elicit this and to help students grow in understanding; not from a blank slate but from integrating prior leaning with the new program. If Casey takes what the students say at face value then she runs the risk of repeating earlier material and not providing a stimulating leaning environment. There is a lot of evidence from contemporary research that young students have a great capacity to grasp key ideas in religious education. The teacher should not underestimate the potential of the student in the RE class.

Think about …
In planning to teach about sacraments and bearing in mind the point about student prior learning, how would you extend the understanding of sacraments by students who show an initial high level of understanding?

Scenario 2: What does this remind you of?

A basic principle of sound teaching in any discipline is to use the experiential world of the student wherever possible. This helps to make learning familiar, and gives students a good introduction to a new area by allowing them to make connections with their own lives. There are many opportunities in RE to make use of students' life experiences. Teaching about reconciliation, for example, throws up a range of possibilities. Use prompt questions like 'When have we felt sorry for something that we have done or not done?' 'How do we make up when we are sorry?' 'How do we feel when someone has hurt or offended us?' Considering these questions is a natural part of life, and students of all ages can enter into a discussion of them based on their own experiences. They are questions which are part of the fabric of life, and it is hard to think of any person who would not have something to contribute.

Think about …
Can you think of some areas under the general heading 'Teaching about Sacraments' that don't really have much overlap with human experience? If so, how would you approach these issues?

Source document 4:
Sofia Cavalletti: The Religious Potential of the Child.

All that we have been able to observe over many years, whether directly or through collaborators and former students, leads us to consider the child as a 'metaphysical' being who moves with ease in the world of the transcendent and who delights in – satisfied and serene – the contact with God. God and the child get along together.

(p. 44)

Questions:
1. Do you agree with this comment? If so, what implications does this have for classroom religious education?
2. Can you think of any examples of God and the child getting along?
3. Does the child ever lose the metaphysical contact with God?

2. Providing the Scaffolding

Most students learn best in an enquiry-based environment. This places great value on students being actively involved in their own learning and taking some responsibility for what goes on in the classroom. At the same time the teacher has a key role to play in providing scaffolding for learning. Scaffolding provides a structure where learning can best take place. Some examples help to highlight what scaffolding learning involves. There are times when student learning is greatly advanced by some direct instruction by the teacher. This is not the dominant mode of classroom interaction but it can be vital in certain circumstances to get around roadblocks or educational dead ends. When teaching about the Eucharist, for example, students' understanding can be greatly enhanced by a clear presentation by the teacher of the idea of Jesus being really present in the form of bread and wine. Students would find this hard to grasp just using their natural reasoning, and it does not have an obvious connection with the experiential world of the child. Once this is presented it allows students to enter into a fuller exploration of the Catholic sense of sacraments. Another example of scaffolding is providing a framework for student directed research. If students are given a strong context for a research task, such as clear instructions on where to look for information, some key resources provided and monitoring to help students stay on task, then the research task should be much more educationally fruitful.

Scenario 3: What do I do?

You are doing a unit on the Last Supper. One of your teaching and learning activities is for students to develop a timeline flowchart of the events before, during and after the Last Supper. As a teacher how would you scaffold this learning?

Think about ...
What skills does an RE teacher need to be able to provide scaffolding for learning?

3. Using Interactive Cooperative Learning Strategies

Students learn best at primary level if they are actively engaged. Strategies which stimulate the use of the senses and call on different skills from the learner should be used whenever possible. A good example of such a technique is the use of Godly Play pedagogy. This approach was discussed in detail in Chapter 5. By an innovative use of Scripture and small stylised figures students are encouraged to learn by playing. This stimulates learning by engaging the imagination of students and helping them make connections between sometimes difficult and disparate concepts. Godly Play can be used in a variety of situations in sacramental units. Another example of an interactive strategy is the use of learning stations. By using a number of areas in the classroom, where different teaching and learning activities are set up and with students moving around them, a variety of learning styles are catered for. Each station may cater for a different learning style and therefore provide a varied experience for students who may appreciate a different approach to a common topic.

Scenario 4: What do I do?

You are doing a unit on Baptism at junior primary level and plan to establish a number of work stations in your class. What activities do you plan to do at each station so as to maximise student involvement and variety of teaching and learning strategies?

Think about …
Why is playing such an effective teaching tool when working with younger students?

FUTHER QUESTIONS AND ACTIVITIES

1. Recall a Sacramental celebration of which you may have been a part, or which you may have observed? Describe this with a partner.

2. Have you been involved with a class of students preparing to celebrate a Sacrament as a part of your teaching practicum? What sorts of activities were the students engaged in?

3. What (if any) concerns do you have in relation to teaching about the Sacraments?

REFERENCES

Gaudium et Spes - Pastoral constitution on the church in the modern world. In A. Flannery (Ed.), *The sixteen basic documents of Vatican Council II (1996)*. Dublin: Dominican Publications.

Catechism of the Catholic church. (1994). Homebush, NSW: St Paul Publications.

Cavaletti, S. (1983). *The religious potential of the child*. New York: Paulist Press.

Grajczonek, J., & Hanifin, P. (2007). Teaching and learning in the early years religion class. In J. Grajczonek & M. Ryan (Eds.), *Religious education in early childhood* (pp. 158–176). Lumino Press: Brisbane.

Hyde, B. (2007). Catechesis of the Good Shepherd: A case study. In J. Grajczonek & M. Ryan (Eds.), *Religious education in early childhood* (pp. 103–115). Lumino Press: Brisbane.

CHAPTER 10

DIMENSIONS OF LEARNING IN RELIGIOUS EDUCATION

A scenario:
Jane is a Year 2 teacher in a Catholic primary school. Today, she is delivering a lesson on the Liturgy, specifically, exploring the parts of the Mass. The intended outcome for this lesson is for the students to be able to describe what happens in the two major parts of the Mass. Jane is extremely well prepared. She has taken great care to become informed about the topic she is teaching, and she has a detailed lesson plan with a series of appropriate learning and teaching strategies. To begin, she revisits the learning from the previous lesson, to which only a few students respond. Then she begins to write up on the chalkboard the two major parts of the Eucharistic celebration – the Liturgy of the Word, the Liturgy of the Eucharist. Jane then begins to try to engage the students by asking them what they might know about each of these major parts of the celebration. However, for most students in the class, there is little connection they can make from this material to their everyday lives. Jane continues to ask constructive questions, and a good effort is made to engage the students. She writes, under each of the headings, some of the things that occur in each part of the Mass, and she has prepared a worksheet, which she now distributes to the students to promote comprehension. By the end of the lesson, the students have been given some information about the two major parts of the Mass, and they were asked to draw and label a picture indicating what happens in these two parts. Jane has, in essence, done all of the appropriate things for this lesson, given the context of the curriculum approach at this school.

Questions:

1. Can you see anything missing in Jane's approach to this RE topic?
2. Why were the students unable to make meaning from the material presented by Jane?
4. What might you do differently?

The scenario above suggests that, although much work has been done in the area of curriculum development in religious education, effective learning and teaching in religious education is not always achieved. At the present time, pedagogical practice is most often represented by outcome based approaches to the curriculum. These have been influential in religious education too. Rather than focusing on the content, outcomes based approaches focus on the knowledge, skills, and understandings which students are expected to acquire. This sounds reasonable. So, why were the students in Jane's lesson unable to make meaning from the material Jane presented? Was the learning model used by Jane in this particular lesson appropriate and effective in engaging the students and in promoting learning?

This chapter explores an appropriate learning model which may assist teachers to develop new perspectives about engaging students through the incorporation of three different, although interconnected aspects of learning: cognitive, affective and spiritual.

THE COGNITIVE DIMENSION

Educators and psychologists today are familiar with the terms, intellectual, cognitive, or rational intelligence. It has a particular focus on the ability to solve problems and to think in an abstract fashion. This notion of intelligence represents the cognitive dimension of learning and is concerned with the acquisition of knowledge, skills and abilities.

Outcomes based approaches to learning and teaching in religious education that focus on the cognitive dimension of learning account for the specific knowledge it is expected that a student will gain by the end of the lesson. For example:

By the end of this lesson students will be able to:
- Name the Church's liturgical colours
- Sequence the parable of the Prodigal Son
- Construct a diorama to create the setting for Sunday Mass
- Compare the stories of Jesus' birth from Matthew and Luke's Gospel
- Recommend one way in which a piece of furniture in the Church could be improved.

Notice that each of the above outcomes states explicitly the knowledge, skills and abilities that students are expected to achieve. Such outcomes use verbs like identify, match, compare, select, plan, critique, construct, and so forth.

Activity 10.1: *Imagine that you are planning a lesson on Holy Week for students in an early years' classroom. List three possible cognitive outcomes that you might include in your lesson.*

A helpful way to frame cognitive outcomes is to think of the type of verb used. This describes the main action of the outcome. However, there are levels of complexity of verbs. Some, such as *name* and *list* describe basic and straightforward tasks. Other, such as *critique* and *hypothesise* involve more elaborate processes. Below is a table comprising verbs adapted from Bloom's taxonomy of cognitive processes. This table is divided into six categories: remembering, understanding, applying, analysing, evaluation, and creating.

Remembering Recognising, recalling, retrieving knowledge from memory, identifying, naming.
Understanding Interpreting, exemplifying, finding a specific example of a concept or principle, classifying, summarizing, comparing, illustrating, categorising, paraphrasing, translating, representing, , predicting, concluding, contrasting, matching.
Applying Executing, implementing, carrying out, using
Analysing Differentiating, distinguishing, organising, selecting, focusing, outlining, structuring, integrating.
Evaluating Checking, critiquing, detecting, testing, coordinating, judging
Creating Generating, planning, producing, hypothesising, designing, constructing

Adapted, Healy, Hyde & Rymarz (2004)

Activity 10.2: *Use some of the terms listed in the table above to create some possible cognitive outcome for students in early years' classrooms.*

However, students seldom learn solely within the cognitive dimension, and many have argued that cognitive knowledge by itself is insufficient to engage students and to ensure that genuine learning has taken place. This, in part, may explain why the students in Jane's RE class in the scenario at the beginning of this chapter were not engaged in their learning. Learning has to *affect* the student. This leads to a second dimension of learning, the affective dimension.

THE AFFETIVE DIMENSION
(EMOTIONAL LEARNING)

The case for a second category of intelligence has been proposed and refined by theorists such as Daniel Goleman (1996). This category is referred to in the literature as Emotional Intelligence (EQ), and is defined as the ability to process emotional information, particularly as it involves perception, assimilation, understanding and management of emotion, that it, its capacity to carry out abstract reasoning, which is a hallmark of intelligence.

Goleman (1996) maintained that cognitive intelligence (IQ) and emotional intelligence (EQ) are not opposing competencies. "These two minds, the emotional and the rational, operate in tight harmony for the most part, intertwining their very different ways of knowing to guide us through the world" (p. 9). He also maintained that one's emotional intelligence is a fundamental requirement for one's effective use of rational intelligence. In other words, a person's feelings play an important role in their thought processes (Hyde, 2003). Consequently, recognising the role of the emotions in the intellectual performance and life of a student should be an important factor in the learning process (de Souza, 2004). This notion of emotional intelligence represents the affective dimension of learning and is concerned with the feelings, reactions and emotions in relation to the content of what is being taught.

Just as it is possible to plan learning that addresses the cognitive dimension it is also possible to devise learning outcomes that address the affective dimension. You will notice as you read on that affective outcomes are difficult to measure because the types of verbs used to write these outcomes are focused on the development of feelings, emotions and reactions. Therefore, they are usually stated in terms of what is desired or hoped for. For example, *by the end of this unit it is hoped that students will...*

- *Appreciate* the importance of Advent for Christians
- *Reflect* on the parable of the Good Samaritan
- *Accept* the need to seek forgiveness and to forgive others

- *Show an awareness* of those who are teased or bullied
- *Develop sensitivity towards* those in need
- *Display an interest* in learning about the features of the Church…

Since the cognitive intelligence (IQ) and emotional intelligence (EQ) operate together, the affective outcomes that are devised should complement the cognitive dimension. If, for example, students are learning about Advent as a season of the Liturgical year, then, at an affective level, it could be hoped that they are developing an appreciation of Advent as a time of waiting in their own lives.

For example:

It is intended that students will identify the themes for each of the four Sundays of Advent (cognitive).

It is hoped that students will begin to appreciate Advent as a time of waiting for Jesus' coming at Christmas in their own lives (affective).

Activity 10.3: *In the previous activity you developed a list of possible cognitive outcomes for a lesson on Holy Week. Write one possible affective outcome to complement these.*

Imagine that you are an early years teacher planning a series of lessons on "Creation". List two possible cognitive and affective outcomes that you might include in your lesson.

THE SPIRITUAL DIMENSION (SPIRITUAL INTELLIGENCE)

A number of writers and theorist in recent times have proposed the existence of a third category of intelligence, known as spiritual intelligence (SQ). Spiritual intelligence, as proposed by Zohar and Marshall (2000) is essential for the effective functioning of both our intellectual quotient (IQ) and emotional quotient (EQ), since, "neither IQ nor EQ, separately or in combination, is enough to explain the full complexity of human intelligence nor the vast richness of the human soul and imagination" (p. 5). de Souza (2006) maintains that the spiritual dimension is therefore a vital factor in the lives of students.

Spirituality is often described as relational (Hay & Nye, 2006) and is demonstrated by a person's expression of connectedness to the human and non-human world. It has been shown to be an innate quality possessed by all human beings (O'Murchu, 1997; Newberg, *et al.*, 2001). Further, Emmons (2000), and Hyde (2004) have argued that a person's spirituality, understood as relationality with self, others, the world, and with a Transcendent dimension (God) can be drawn upon by the individual as a form of intelligence.

Spiritual intelligence, according to Zohar and Marshall (2000) is the mental aptitude used by human beings to address and find solutions to problems of meaning and value, and to place their lives and actions into a wider, richer, meaning-giving context. It has to do with a *relational component* to one's life.

de Souza (2006) argues that while rational intelligence (IQ) and emotional intelligence correspond to the cognitive and affective dimensions respectively, spiritual intelligence corresponds to the spiritual/inner reflective dimension. While the theories of these three intelligences have attracted both support and criticism, they do provide a rationale and a framework to consider the development of learning programs that address the three aspects of being: rational (thinking), emotional (feeling) and spiritual (inner reflection).

In the same way that it has been possible to devise learning outcome for the cognitive and affective dimensions, it is also possible to plan learning outcomes for the spiritual dimension of learning. Such outcomes address the inner reflecting of the student, usually with a focus on an outward expression. This indicates not only that the intellect and the emotions have worked together to produce a deeper level of engagement, but that the learning has gone beyond the surface. It has reached the core where the learning becomes transformed by an inner response which may and should lead to outward expressions of changed thinking and behaviour (de Souza, 2004).

Examples of spiritual outcomes could include the following:

*It is hoped that students will **reflect inwardly** to decide upon ways in which they can act as carers for God's creation.*

*It is hoped that students will **accept responsibility** for the choices they make.*

*It is hoped that students will **develop compassion** for those who are teased or bullied.*

Other verbs that can be used to write spiritual outcomes could include:

- Contemplate
- Empathize
- Meditate
- Show commitment to…
- Display awe and wonder
- Become more deeply involved in…
- Show consideration for…
- Express concern
- Feel connected to

de Souza (2004, 2006) has undertaken much work in relation to developing a curriculum model for education which brings together these three dimensions of learning. The following figure is an adaptation of de Souza's original model, and represents a conceptualisation of a learning model for addressing the cognitive, affective and spiritual dimensions of the curriculum.

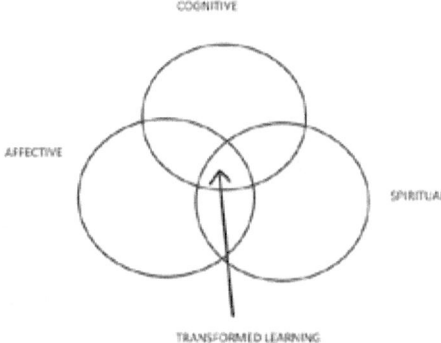

Each circle represents one of the dimensions of learning – cognitive, affective and spiritual. Any of these could be the entry point for students' learning. The middle section, where all three circles intersect represents the point where learning has gone beyond the surface to reach the core, and may become transformed. That is, the learning has addressed the cognitive, affective and spiritual dimensions, and has resulted in an outward expression of thinking or behaviour.

Activity 10.4: *Consider the cognitive and affective outcomes you have developed for the sequence of lessons on Holy Week. Write one spiritual outcome that complements both of these.*

CONCLUSION

It is important to recognise the interconnectedness of these three dimensions of learning, and to plan to address each dimension within the religious education curriculum. Devising learning outcomes to address each of these dimensions is one way to ensure that they are covered within the lesson or unit of work. Although the affective and spiritual dimensions may not be demonstrable, or measurable, statements about them help to ensure that teachers will keep these three areas in mind and they plan and teach (de Souza, 2004). A key way that is achieved is through devising learning and teaching experiences that address these outcomes. In this way, learning becomes more holistic and less fragmented.

FURTHER QUESTIONS AND ACTIVITIES

1. If you were Jane, the teacher in the scenario at the beginning of this chapter, what outcomes might to devise to address the cognitive, affective and spiritual dimensions of learning so as to engage the students?

2. What types of learning and teaching activities might you devise, if were Jane, to enable students to achieve these outcomes?

3. Look at the figure of the learning model presented in this chapter. Does it make sense to you? What might some of the challenges be in implementing such a model to guide your learning and teaching?

4. Imagine that you are devising a unit of work which focuses on the broad topic of "Jesus". Devise one possible cognitive, affective and spiritual outcome for this topic.

5. Now, devise two or three possible learning and teaching activities that may assist students to achieve the above learning outcomes.

REFERENCES

de Souza, M. (2004). Teaching for effective learning in religious education: A discussion of the perceiving, thinking, feeling and intuiting elements in the learning process. *Journal of Religious Education, 52* (3), 22-30.

de Souza, M. (2006). Rediscovering the spiritual dimension in education: Promoting a sense of self and place, meaning and purpose in learning. In M. de Souza, G. Durka, K. Engebretson, R. Jackson, & A. McGrady (Eds.), *International handbook of the religious, moral and spiritual dimensions in education* (pp. 1127-1139). Dordrecht, The Neverland: Springer.

Emmons, R. (2000). Is spirituality an intelligence? Motivation, cognition, and the psychology of ultimate concerns. *The international Journal for the Psychology of Religion, 10* (1), 3-26.

Goleman, D. (1995). *Emotional intelligence: Why it can matter more than IQ*. London: Bloomsbury.

Hay, D., & Nye, R. (2006). *The spirit of the child* (2nd ed.). London: Jessica Kingsley.

Healy, H., Hyde, B., & Rymarz, R. (2004). *Making our way through primary RE: A handbook for religious educators*. Tuggerah, NSW: Social Science Press.

Hyde, B. (2003). Spiritual intelligence: A critique. *Journal of Religious Education, 51* (1), 13-20.

Hyde, B. (2004). The plausibility of spiritual intelligence: Spiritual experience, problem solving, and neural sites. *International Journal of Children's Spirituality, 9* (1), 39-52.

Newberg, A., d'Aquili, E., & Rause, V. (2001). *Why God won't go away: Brain science and the biology of belief*. New York: Ballantine.

O'Murchu, D. (1997). *Reclaiming spirituality: A new spiritual framework for today's world*. Dublin: Gateway.

Zohar, D., & Marshall, I. (2000). *SQ. Spiritual intelligence: The ultimate intelligence*. London: Bloomsbury.

www.ingramcontent.com/pod-product-compliance
Lightning Source LLC
Chambersburg PA
CBHW021859230426
43671CB00006B/453